TOTAL TEACHING

Your Passion Makes It Happen

Tom Staszewski

Rowman & Littlefield Education
Lanham, Maryland • Toronto • Plymouth, UK
2008

Published in the United States of America
by Rowman & Littlefield Education
A Division of Rowman & Littlefield Publishers, Inc.
A wholly owned subsidiary of The Rowman & Littlefield Publishing Group, Inc.
4501 Forbes Boulevard, Suite 200, Lanham, Maryland 20706
www.rowmaneducation.com

Estover Road
Plymouth PL6 7PY
United Kingdom

British Library Cataloguing in Publication Information Available

Library of Congress Cataloging-in-Publication Data
Staszewski, Tom, 1952–
   Total teaching : your passion makes it happen / Tom Staszewski.
     p. cm.
   Includes bibliographical references.
   ISBN-13: 978-1-57886-704-2 (hardcover : alk. paper)
   ISBN-10: 1-57886-704-5 (hardcover : alk. paper)
   ISBN-13: 978-1-57886-705-9 (pbk. : alk. paper)
   ISBN-10: 1-57886-705-3 (pbk. : alk. paper)
   1. Effective teaching. 2. Motivation in education. 3. Teachers–Conduct of
life. I. Title.
LB1025.3.S7335 2008
371.102–dc22   2007030648

CONTENTS

Acknowledgments   vii

Introduction   ix

1 Today's Teacher   1
   Teaching As a Career Choice   5
   Current Events in Education   9
   Unfounded, Unjustified Criticism   11
   Teacher Advocacy   11
   Tom Monzo, Jr., Third Grade Teacher   16
   Today's Real Unsung Heroes   17

2 The Attributes of a Teacher   20
   A Passion for Teaching   22
   Why Did You Become a Teacher?   22
   Light the Flame Within   23

3 Classroom Success   26
   Self-Talk: Positive Word Usage and Affirmations   28
   Self-Talk for a More Successful Year or 180 Days and Counting   32
   How to Be More Energetic and Enthusiastic   36

Overcoming the Urge to Procrastinate   38
Learning How to Say "No" (and Feel Good about It)   40

4 Motivation   43
Goal Setting   44
Brainstorming   47
Time Management Techniques   48
Sometimes You Just Have to Make the Time   52
The Paperwork Avalanche   54
How to Complete a Major Project   54

5 Creativity   60
Ways to Enhance Your Own Creativity   62
Movies, Entertainment, and Filmmaking   63
Music   64
Humor—You Have to Laugh!   66
When All Else Fails, Sometimes You Just Have to Laugh!   70
Ways to Create Humor in the Classroom   71

6 Change   73
Overcoming Adversity and Difficult Times   75
Life's Lessons   77
Memorable Events   82
Stress Relief   83
Stress in the Classroom   85
Take a Deep Breath   86
How to Stay Calm under Pressure   87
Self Rehab   89
Journal Writing: Why You Should Have Your Own Journal   89
Remember the Importance of Play   92
What Do You Do for Fun?   93
Remember to Say "Thank You"   94

7 Take Care of Yourself   96
Your Ideal Level of Performance—Being Your Best   97
Physical Fitness   100
Parking Lot Paradox   104
Getting Started   105
Diet   106
Take Care of Your Voice   112

8 You're Never Too Old to Teach   118
      Thoughts about Longevity and the Aging Process   121
      Planning to Retire?   125

9 Summary and Commentary   128
      A Positive Change: Momentum Gaining on
          Teacher Recognition   130
      One Last Assignment: Give Your Teachers An A+   131

Appendix: Reference Quotes and Worksheet   133

About the Author   143

ACKNOWLEDGMENTS

I extend my sincere appreciation and gratitude to God and to all those who encouraged and assisted me in the writing of this book. Along the way to completing this project were many individuals, friends, associates, and colleagues too numerous to name who provided me with energy and encouragement.

To all of the teachers who taught me, I am indebted to their expertise, patience, guidance, and support they provided throughout all of my experiences as a student. In particular, Coach Ed Onoroto, Coach Donald Zonno, and memorable teachers, such as Larry Behan, Billy Kleiner, Pat Ciotti, Walter Helminski, Dr. John Weidman, Dr. Glenn Nelson, and Dr. Peg Mahler.

My mother and father were also instrumental in the pursuit of my academic endeavors. I am forever indebted for their love, guidance, and enduring support. My parents always stressed that education is the best investment possible because it will open doors of opportunity and no one can take away knowledge once it is acquired.

Finally, and most importantly, my wife and best friend, Linda Laird Staszewski deserves my most heartfelt thanks, love, and admiration for always being there.

INTRODUCTION

Teaching today is certainly demanding. You don't need this book to remind you of that. Beyond your typical concerns about curricula, classroom management, planning, paperwork, and your ever-growing things-to-do list, you are now living in an era of profound educational reform. Pressure and change abound in today's educational environments. Reform movements such as charter schools, vouchers, home-schooling, privatization efforts, statewide high-stakes testing, either not enough or too much parental involvement, ever-changing governmental regulations, the impact of new technology, and now even the anticipation of nationwide standards have created a whole new look to the teaching profession.

Enough, already! Or so you hope. Well, don't count on it. Change is apparent everywhere, and throughout all levels of education, rumblings are being heard. So, before you put this book down, thinking that you've heard all this before, let me clarify my point. By mentioning the reform movements and accountability measures, I just want to acknowledge the fact that I realize that you are under greater scrutiny than ever before. Your role as a teacher is being examined more closely at many levels: by parents and supervisors at the local level, governors and lawmakers at the state level, policy makers and politicians at the national level, and the media at all levels. It seems that nowadays, everyone has an opinion about schools and schoolteachers. With all of these concerns, I offer this book as a means of assisting you to "rise above and go beyond" all of the current issues that we, as educators, are faced with.

This book is about teachers and for teachers, but it is not really about teaching. It is designed to assist you in handling all of the issues I have mentioned, help you to be better able to respond and move ahead as a more effective individual, and, ultimately, enhance your role as a teacher. This book is not about teaching strategies or techniques; it is not about curricula or methodologies. What it *is* about is you. You as an individual. You as a person. And as a member of the noblest profession, how you can accomplish all of your hopes and aspirations. This book also addresses the unlimited human potential that we all possess. It recognizes the special uniqueness in you. It acknowledges that there are proven ways to act in the face of change rather than react to it, that there are proven methods for becoming the best that we can, and that there are ways for us to use our potential and achieve greatness in our lives and in our daily activities.

So, you could say that this book is about life, and about living. It is a validation of the teaching profession, which recognizes the premise that "teaching is the profession that has created all other professions." Yet, this book does not deal with methodologies; it deals with ways to increase your potential and to become the best possible teacher that you can. It will provide you with a means of discovering who you are and what you want to accomplish both as a teacher and as a whole person.

Ideally, you should be able to integrate the various aspects in your life: physical, mental, family, social, spiritual, and whatever other areas of your life are important to you. So as you read this book, look for the inspiration on living your life because after all, you know that teaching is not just a job, but a way of life. Therefore, your way of life will be the focal point of this writing. Together we will look at ways to enhance the quality of life for you and those around you. You will learn to use more of your potential. It is commonly accepted that the average person uses only 10–15 percent of their power, potential, and resources. We will take a look at that other 85–90 percent of your talents, potential, and strengths that are just waiting there for you to use. So, get ready to unlock your potential.

This journey into greatness, in many respects, will be a do-it-yourself project, for within you lies all of the resources that you need. This book will be a catalyst to help you tap those assets. And, ultimately, you and your students will be the ones who benefit.

❶

TODAY'S TEACHER

An attempt to capture the duties and responsibilities of a teacher in a job description may look something like this:

TEACHER WANTED

A trained professional with a bachelor's degree required, master's degree preferred. Must have content and subject matter expertise to teach math, reading, writing, and life skills to as many as 30+ children at any given moment. Many of the students have severe behavioral problems, and some have limited knowledge of English usage. Some students have problems with alcohol and other drugs, emotional and psychological difficulties, learning disabilities, or attention deficit disorder, or suffer from abuse and other adverse home and socioeconomic conditions. The applicant should be able to maintain discipline and classroom management at all times without using force or physical intervention.

In addition to teaching subject matter and content areas, the applicant must offset any suspected substance abuse and teach the biological functions of the sexual reproduction system while advocating sexual abstinence. Personal religious beliefs and practices will not be permitted. Individual

(continued)

---

should be familiar with basic legal and law enforcement procedures and regulations.

The position is accountable to the school board, school principal, numerous politicians, taxpayers, parent groups, various committees, union officials, concerned media, the superintendent, and the general public. Applicants must prepare each and every student to successfully pass a multitude of state and national high-stakes tests and make annual yearly progress or be subject to punitive measures or dismissal.

In addition, a whole host of other tasks need to be done when you are a teacher. Just think of all you have to do—today's teacher is faced with a seemingly insurmountable workload that includes: the design and implementation of curriculum; completion and submission of daily lesson plans; fulfilling curriculum objectives with each lesson; implementing technology; taking attendance; documenting student progress; submitting progress reports; completing individualized education programs; writing and receiving referrals; meeting with colleagues; scheduling parent conferences; attending faculty meetings, in-service, and professional development training; earning a graduate degree; serving on committees; learning the newest methodologies; correcting homework; designing bulletin boards; completing report cards; supervising hall duty; monitoring the cafeteria and playground; conducting fire drills; assisting in bus duty; tutoring students; many other related duties, and a multitude of unexpected related or unrelated necessities that may arise.

If that's not enough—because of ever-increasing budget shortfalls, many teachers dip into their own pockets and regularly spend money on classroom supplies and resources for their students.

In a March 9, 2002 article in the *Erie Times News*,[1] The National School Supply and Equipment Association reported that individually, teachers spend $589 annually on school supplies and equipment. It is a hidden bill that is expected and accepted. Critics of our school systems often overlook these expenditures. I have often wondered just how much an outspoken critic would be willing to spend to do his or her job—probably nothing. In the private sector and corporate world, it is unheard of for employees to have to buy job-related materials, supplies, and equipment out of their own pockets. Imagine an administrative assistant required to bring a personal computer to work or a truck driver buying his or her own gasoline!

On the other hand, teachers know that these expenses are justified because they are beneficial to their students and help to improve their overall effectiveness. Teachers who regularly spend their own money should be commended and recognized for their extra efforts.

Instead of acknowledging that teachers willingly spend their own money on classroom materials, critics will often focus on the supposedly shortened workday that teachers enjoy. Still others claim, "Yes, teachers are busy, but at least they get a planning period each day to get things done." Well, you know the so-called planning period is really a misnomer. Many times you are so involved with the day's activities that there is no time to stop and plan. Even if you are entitled to that one period, chances are it's already been expended with the unexpected. Many times your building principal may have other plans for your planning period. I've often wondered why they even bothered to call it a planning period. Planning? Those precious minutes that are supposed to be devoted to planning are often filled with endless amounts of paperwork, meetings, interruptions, schedule changes, extra assigned duties, phone calls, conferences, gathering missed work for absent students, completing forms, submitting required data, and on and on. Maybe they call it a planning period, because there's no time left for planning . . . period.

You might find it interesting to see how the government defines teaching. The U.S. Department of Labor's *Dictionary of Occupational Titles*[2] is a publication that defines and indexes over 20,000 job titles. Often referred to as the DOT, the dictionary categorizes jobs, describes the training and education necessary for the job, details the duties and responsibilities, and lists the respective wages (p. 4).

Makes you wonder who would want a job like this. Well, in spite of all the hardships associated with teaching and the downside that comes with being a teacher, there is the upside: the gratifying aspects of our profession. After parents and families, teachers have one of the most important roles in helping children realize their potential. Once children leave their homes and enter their school, this awesome responsibility suddenly rests with you.

As you teach, a kind of magic occurs in the classroom. You know the feeling. It's when the connection finally occurs, when the lesson you are teaching finally clicks and makes sense and then the thrill of learning

TEACHER, ELEMENTARY SCHOOL, DOT# 092.227-010

Teaches elementary school students academic, social, and motor skills in public or private schools: Prepares course objectives and an outline for course of study following curriculum guidelines or requirements of state and school. Lectures, demonstrates, and uses audiovisual teaching aids to present subject matter to class. Prepares, administers, and corrects tests, and records results. Assigns lessons, corrects papers, and hears oral presentations. Teaches rules of conduct. Maintains order in classroom and on playground. Counsels pupils when adjustment and academic problems arise. Discusses pupils' academic and behavior and behavioral attitudes and achievements with parents. Keeps attendance and grade records as required by school. May coordinate class field trips. May teach combined grade classes. May specialize by subject taught, such as math, science, or social studies. May be required to hold state certification.

TEACHER, SECONDARY SCHOOL, DOT# 092.227-010

Teaches one or more subjects to students in public or private secondary schools. Instructs students, using various teaching methods, such as lecture and demonstration, and uses audiovisual aids and other materials to supplement presentations. Prepares course objectives and an outline for course of study following curriculum guidelines or requirements of state and school. Assigns lessons and corrects homework. Administers tests to evaluate pupil progress, records results, and issues reports to inform parents of progress. Keeps attendance records. Maintains discipline in classroom. Meets with parents to discuss student progress and problems. Participates in faculty and professional meetings, educational conferences, and teacher training workshops. Performs related duties, such as sponsoring one or more activities or student organizations, assisting pupils in selecting course of study, and counseling students with adjustment and academic problems. May be required to hold certification from state.

and the exuberant experience of education catches a hold of your students. You can see it in their eyes as they begin to experience the zest of learning and the transformation that magically happens as the lesson takes hold. It truly is a magical moment when that breakthrough finally occurs, and you've reached that student.

You should be feeling good about the role you play and the lasting contribution you make in the lives of your students. After a good day at school, you should feel glad about the important work that you do. Consequently, after a bad day, you can reinspire yourself as you focus on the overall good that you do. It is important to keep your days in proper perspective and to sort out the difficult days by reminding yourself of the big picture and value of your teaching. You can gain further inspiration by reminding yourself why you joined the profession in the first place. Keep your attitude focused on that reason and you'll be better able to cope with the difficult days.

You fully know what your job entails and all that you have to do in a typical day. Although, with each day being so different and the unexpected occurring at any given time, there probably is nothing like a typical day.

TEACHING AS A CAREER CHOICE

The teaching profession contains a paradox. Across the country, there is a divergence between those who are leaving the teaching profession and those that want to become teachers. You've probably noticed it yourself, too. Perhaps, this situation may pertain to you. Which category do you find yourself in at the present moment?

- ☐ A brand-new teacher, having just entered the profession and begun your first professional career—a recent college graduate
- ☐ A career teacher with_____number of years behind you
- ☐ A current teacher who is anticipating to retire in another year or two
- ☐ A current teacher contemplating taking an early retirement
- ☐ A "first-time teacher," one who has had other careers but always wanted to be a teacher
- ☐ A recently retired individual who now wants to start a brand-new career as a teacher
- ☐ An individual with a bachelor's degree pursing an alternative certification program
- ☐ A beginning teacher, in the first three to five years of teaching

Regardless of what category you find yourself in, there are ideas and recommendations in this book that are designed to help you. I believe that whatever situation you find yourself in, you will be able to learn more about yourself and your potential, obtain some excellent tips, strategies, and techniques to be more effective in the classroom and, most importantly, in all aspects of your life.

Recently, while doing some in-service instruction at an elementary school, I met a man who had just turned 50. Matt was serving as a student teacher, having just completed his bachelor's degree from a local university. He was in the process of obtaining the necessary state certification so he could become a bona fide member of the teaching profession. As I observed Matt, I was impressed with his sincere dedication and commitment that he displayed toward his students. Later on, as I spent some time in the faculty room talking with other teachers, I was able to observe the mutual respect and collegiality that existed between the brand-new, 20-something teachers, the veterans of the building, and the 50-year-old rookie. All of the various categories of teachers were comingling and interacting in a true spirit of professionalism and cooperation.

I believe that this kind of interaction is occurring throughout the country. Many states have an extreme shortage of teachers, and in other states, a teacher surplus. Today, there are many individuals who have decided to enter the teaching profession later on in their lives. It is becoming common to see first-time teachers who are in their 40s, 50s, and, yes, even 60s.

Many diverse paths lead to teaching. Today's new teachers often have a wide variety of backgrounds and experiences. The current teacher shortage and changes in certification policies and requirements have led schools to place teachers with varying levels of preparation. Many beginning teachers have completed the traditional route of college or university education programs. These teacher education programs usually include extensive academic course work and a semester of student teaching. Many other new teachers have completed full-year internships under the tutelage of a master teacher in a structured professional development school. In addition, many others are entering teaching through special alternative certification programs. Often, these special certification programs have only a short orientation component. It is also becoming commonplace to see an increasing number of individuals joining the teaching ranks with no preparation at all. These emergency certificates have opened the door to full-time teaching assignments.

If, on the other hand, you are new to the profession after having been in another field, this book can be of assistance to you, too. Many transplanted teachers from other professions are surprised about how much stamina and endurance it takes to teach. In order to make it through the day, it's almost like running a marathon.

Another important category of teachers are those recent college graduates who, during the first three to five years of teaching, decide to stop teaching and walk away from the profession. This segment of the teaching population is responsible for much of the current shortages. The disillusioned teacher who decides that there are greener pastures outside the classroom quickly becomes dissatisfied and resigns. If you find yourself contemplating to leave teaching, please carefully review your decision. Granted, no one ever promised you a bed of roses, but please reconsider, because we need you. Your services are greatly needed to offset the predicted shortage. Of course, I am not dismissing your concerns or discounting why you may want to leave. I just want you to know that there are some ideas here that you can use to make your job more fulfilling. This book can provide you with the needed boost or catalyst to hang in there and make the best of your situation. I'm convinced that, as a national issue, we should concentrate more on retaining the teachers who are already working while continuing to train new recruits.

Many disillusioned teachers that I have talked with have indicated that their dissatisfaction comes from such things as low pay, student misbehavior, lack of parental involvement, and lack of support from administration. Although it may be necessary to improve the job conditions, often, the only thing we have control over is our own attitudes and our responses to the situations we are faced with. Most teachers leave during their first five years in the classroom, not near the end of their careers. After five years, the departure rates start to level off. So, the five-year plan seems to be a factor in making it as a career teacher. Being able to make it through the first five years is the barrier that needs to be broken to allow teaching to be a lasting, long-term career.

So, before you decide to take another job, be sure that you give it some time and fully consider your choices. You know that the grass is not always greener. This book can help you to realize that often we need to change ourselves, rather than change our situations or try to change someone else. You and I are in control of ourselves, and we can be the

masters of our own destinations and create the conditions that will motivate us.

In order to fill the increasing numbers of teaching vacancies, most
states provide alternative certification programs. Many newspaper articles around the country are addressing the widespread teacher shortage. This shortage is likely to become more prevalent in the next
decade. The result has been that some undertrained teachers have already been placed in the classroom. For the past several years, federal,
state, and local officials have been working to cut red tape and make it
easier for prospective teachers—especially those entering teaching as a
second career—to get the training they need to enter the classroom as
quickly as possible. In 1983, only 8 states had alternative certification
programs; today, 45 states have them.

Mainstream media loves to cover topics related to teaching. An Ann
Landers column from March 20, 2002[3] featured how gratifying a "second career" as a teacher was for one individual. The letter referred to
the writer's husband who was laid off from a business job when he was
59 years old. At first he volunteered at a local elementary school and discovered that he enjoyed working with children. Since he had a bachelor's degree, he was easily able to become a substitute teacher. He then
took additional classes and became a certified teacher. Now, at 70, he
was in his fifth year as a master teacher with full tenure. The writer indicated that her husband was happier as a teacher than he ever had been
as an executive.

Another column featured a 25-year career attorney who decided to
become a teacher. However, in this particular case, the "career switcher"
soon returned to practicing law after just a half-year of teaching. He
didn't realize how demanding teaching could be. Although he dreamed
of being a teacher, he didn't anticipate all of the duties that were associated with the profession. He was not prepared for all of the challenges
and conditions of the normal related tasks, such as writing lesson plans,
grading assignments and exams, doing daily evaluations, demanding administrative tasks, endless paperwork, frequent meetings, and accu-
rately preparing and following individualized education programs. It
wasn't the cushy job with time off during the summer that he anticipated. Classroom management was not all about gum-chewing infrac-
tions. Whereas one individual found teaching to be a very rewarding and

gratifying second career, the other individual, after spending a half-year of 14-hour days as a teacher, became disillusioned and returned to his first career as a lawyer. I know that there are many other examples of second-career teachers both relishing and regretting their decisions. Either way, I think it's important to perform a lot of soul searching and self-examination when considering a teaching career.

CURRENT EVENTS IN EDUCATION

Although this book does not deal with any specific approaches to teaching and learning, it is important, though, to have an understanding about current issues and trends in education. The amount of change occurring in the field of education is significant, and today's teacher, to be truly effective, needs to keep current of all the critical issues in education. I highly recommend that you take the time to see what the current issues and trends are and how they affect your position.

As a former middle school social studies teacher, I have a passion for current events. It is vitally important for me to know what is going on. For over 30 years, it has been my practice to read 5 daily newspapers and at least 3 Sunday newspapers every week. I make it a point to know what is happening at the local, state, national, and global levels. I also invest in numerous journals, newsletters, e-mail list serves, periodicals, and other related publications. This working knowledge and understanding of educational issues is an essential part of my profession. The amount of coverage that education has in today's mainstream publications is truly amazing. It is very common to see articles on educational issues and trends that were previously relegated to some obscure journal or research publication now on today's front page.

Years ago, I was reminded of the importance of knowing what was going on in education. I was facilitating a staff development training session for a large, countywide educational services agency, and each day I noticed a support staff person clipping newspaper articles. Having a fondness for current events, I couldn't help but ask her what she was doing. She explained that the organization subscribed to six daily newspapers and that it was her responsibility to go through each publication, page by page, to find any articles related to education. She would clip, copy, and send them in a daily packet to every administrator at the agency. She said it was important for them to be aware of matters related to education. That had a tremendous impact on me. I was quite impressed about how astute those administrators were and how essential it was to know about the world of education.

With today's technology, web-based publications, and e-mail subscriptions, the method of obtaining educational news has changed and become more streamlined. A number of online publications can now provide this kind of service. Even if you still peruse the daily papers, I urge you to seek out information on educational issues on a daily basis. The more working knowledge you have, the more solid foundation you have about what is happening in our profession. Do so, and you will be better able to adjust and adapt to the rapid changes that are occurring. This will then enable you to act rather than react, and be in a better position to deal with all of the uncertainty that can surround us, as teachers.

Another part of my professional background included teaching in an adult education/employment and training center. Our students consisted of adult learners who were economically disadvantaged, unemployed, or underemployed, as well as those who were welfare clients. At that time, our state and national government had implemented a variety of welfare reform measures that substantially changed the nature of such programs. I remember that many of the students had no knowledge whatsoever that reform movements were underway and, all too often, were caught by surprise. They suddenly found themselves faced with drastic changes to their benefits and new limitations on their eligibility for related services. The welfare reform movement took decades to implement and changes were announced often five years in advance, and still many clients were unaware of the changes even as they occurred. Had they followed the trends and shifts in the policies, they could have prepared to take the necessary action to get ready for the dramatic changes.

One of my favorite courses that I teach at the graduate level is "Current Issues in Education." Teachers often enrolled in this graduate course are quite surprised when they discover all the new changes. Sorting through all of the legislative changes and educational reform movements can be quite a monumental task. Many of the graduate students who take this course are full-time teachers who find themselves faced with a multitude of trends and issues. Some of my students have little or no initial knowledge about such issues as charter schools, vouchers, re-constitution, privatization efforts, proprietary schools, political agendas, high-stakes testing, legislative mandates, or school funding issues. It is very easy for a teacher to lose focus on the big picture of education by concentrating only on the four walls of the classroom. My point is that today's educator needs to know the impact that reform movements will have on them, their students, their communities, and their schools.

UNFOUNDED, UNJUSTIFIED CRITICISM

Do you remember the headlines from 1993 National Adult Literacy Survey announcing that "40 Million People in America Can't Read This," and "One in Five High School Graduates Could Not Read Their Diplomas"? Guess what? Those reports were wrong. It was later determined that only 5 percent, not the previously reported 20 percent, of adults could not read.[4]

I believe a lot of antagonism toward teachers arose as a result of that 1993 federal study. Many Americans became disillusioned with our school systems and began to wonder what was wrong. The avalanche of criticism leveled at our schools and particularly the backlash against public school teachers is often based on the reports of low test scores and lack of skills. I vividly recall several politicians denouncing the public school systems by saying that "one in five high school graduates could not read their diplomas," as they demanded educational reform and teacher accountability.

That damage and the unfair, unjust, and unfounded criticism have severely harmed the reputation of our schools and cast doubt on the teacher's ability to teach.

TEACHER ADVOCACY

Today's teachers are in need of all the recognition, accolades, tributes, and acknowledgment that can be bestowed upon them. Teachers truly deserve a sincere "thank you" for all the tremendous benefits they provide society.

More of an effort should be made to publicize the expanded roles that teachers are now providing. In addition to teaching the designated subject matter and covering all the content areas, teachers are now wearing multiple hats in all daily endeavors. As you well know, teachers' duties have now grown to the added dimensions of counselor, mentor, coach, resource person, mediator, enforcer, and life-long student.

Unfortunately, not all people are aware of the good work that teachers do and the expanded services they provide. Education has recently had more than its share of critics who like to take regular potshots at today's schools and its teachers. I firmly believe that these individuals would not last a couple of hours doing the kind of work teachers do, mainly because they do not understand the real job of a teacher.

There was a very vocal critic who prided himself in bashing teachers. It was very common to see his scathing Letters to the Editor condemning just about everything that teachers do. Other letters went on about how anyone can teach, and that teachers are underworked, overpaid, and not deserving of having summers and holiday breaks off. I am sure that you know someone like this person, someone who has a distorted, unfounded, unrealistic view of the demanding schedule and important duties you actually have.

Well, one day our critic got a big surprise. A wise middle school principal actually invited the critic to spend a day in the school, and the critic took him up on it. And it was not just a sit-back-and-observe kind of day—he got a day in the life of a typical classroom teacher.

Here was his itinerary in a nutshell:

8:00: Homeroom: Take roll. Try to prevent a petty argument from escalating into a real fight. Assist a sick student and send her to the nurse.

8:30: First period through third: follow the group from class to class—history, algebra, and P.E.

10:15: Hall duty: Much confusion. Shoving. Inappropriate language. One student was sent to the principal for dress-code violation.

11:35: Cafeteria duty: Food is thrown. Student was sent to office. A tray was dropped—big mess with spilled milk; paper towels absorbed liquid until maintenance is called.

12:00: Lunch: He tried to pace himself to make it through the day because he hadn't had more than a five-minute break between classes. He was glad when his own lunch period began, and he tried to sneak off to a nearby restaurant. Instead, the principal gave him a bagged lunch and he headed toward the teachers' lounge.

12:35: Bathroom monitor: Two boys caught smoking. Toilet was clogged; no toilet paper.

1:40: Escorted class to weekly assembly in auditorium.

2:15: Bus duty: Oversaw the safe, successful filling of 15 buses. Only one minor fall, no big injuries, but sent student to the nurse to make sure. Only three students missed their buses and had to call home.

To say the least, he was quite surprised. The teachers knew exactly who he was and why he was there, yet they were civil to him nonetheless. But often, they were too busy to even notice his presence. Most teachers inhaled their lunches while returning phone calls to parents who could be reached at that time of the day. They photocopied, graded papers, and prepped for the next lesson while eating. The visitor thought he could at least take a quiet break to relax, but there was just too much going on in the teachers' lounge.

By the end of the day, the critic just didn't look the same. His tie was off and neck collar wide open, perspiration stained his shirt, and his hair was a mess. When someone spoke to him unexpectedly, he froze up like a frightened animal. At the end of his day, he crumbled into the chair in the principal's office and said, "This *is* extremely difficult, isn't it?"

Too many people have the mistaken notion that anyone can teach. Going to school is probably the one common denominator that most people have; however, in their limited vision, they have observed and experienced only a fraction of what schools are like. They never saw behind the scenes; they just walked into a clean, prepared classroom in the morning and began to learn. They think that they can teach because they saw other people teach.

Yet, when looking at other professions and occupations, these same people are content with the knowledge that they can't perform those jobs. They might have seen the cockpit of an airplane, but they don't assume that they can fly it. They know and understand the court system, but don't believe that they can practice law. They certainly don't think they are able to perform surgery. In many cases, the amount of time spent preparing to be a teacher and maintaining certification is nearly the same as the pilot, lawyer, or healthcare professional.

Every day in the career of a teacher is hectic and full of countless interpersonal exchanges. The following is a typical Monday to try to explain the complexity of a teacher's day; this is an actual day in the life of a current teacher in the Pittsburgh, Pennylsvania, area.

7:30: Drop my children off at daycare as early as possible.

8:00: Arrive at school. Several teachers stop me on the way to my room to ask me about my weekend. I try not to be brief, but there is work to be done before the kids get here. There is very little time for small talk.

8:10: I arrive at my room. I have 20 minutes to organize my thoughts, check my lesson plans for the day, and make copies. I discover copies are needed for five classes. I must have been too burned-out last Friday to do this before I left.

8:15: I'm now in line at the copier. There are four teachers in front of me. I decide to get a cup of coffee in the teacher's room and use the slower copier.

8:20: I arrive in the teacher's room. As usual, the other copier is broke and no one has made any coffee. I put on a pot of coffee and head back to the other copier to stand in line.

8:25: I'm back in line at the other copier. There are now six teachers in front of me. I decide to give up on the copying for now and get some coffee instead.

8:30: I get my cup of coffee. I have little time to enjoy it because the kids are arriving and I can't take it back to my classroom.

8:35: I am back in my classroom and the kids are arriving. I put writing prompts up on the board. A student comes up behind me and says he's sick. I send him to the nurse. Another student arrives and tells me he forgot his lunch money. I send him to call his mom. Another student has forgotten her book bag (left it at home) and needs a pencil. I lend her one for the day. The room is now half full and buzzing with activity.

8:50: Another teacher needs to see me in the hall. He just received a note from a parent. The note is for me about last Friday's science test. It reads, "Johnny did not have time to study for his science test or complete #17–20. I do not want him punished for this! There was entirely too much sent home tonight, and giving NO notice for a chapter test is completely unfair. I have asked again and again to be given sufficient notice for tests and quizzes so Johnny has time to reread the material and learn it instead of memorize it. I honestly don't understand why teachers refuse to help parents teach their children to plan ahead and develop good study habits. Please call me on your break."

Regardless, we spent two weeks preparing for this "open book test," which included two quizzes, two experiments, a chapter review, and a review game.

9:00: Take attendance, take the lunch count, and lead the students to Music class.

9:05: Drop the students off at Music class and head back to the copier.

9:10: Make copies for five classes. Call the irate parent back, but she's already on her way to work. I'll call her at lunchtime. Finish that cold cup of coffee and head back to get the students from Music class.

9:35: Reading class: introduce the new vocabulary words, introduce the new spelling words, and complete four workbook pages.

10:00: Bathroom break. Lead all students to the bathroom and then for a drink of water. While they are at the water fountain, I sneak back into the teacher's room to use the bathroom since I didn't have time to go earlier.

10:05: Finish Reading class and prepare for Science class, which I will teach three times today.

10:30: Begin Science class. We're having an experiment today, and even though it is a new Science series, I have provided over half of the materials needed for three classes.

11:10: Prepare for lunch. Lead the students to lunch. Hurry to the teacher's room. Eat lunch and get ready for recess duty. Call the parent back, but she's not available.

11:40: Pick the students up from lunch and go to recess. A student falls off of the monkey bars and breaks his arm. I rush him to the nurse. His mother arrives and takes him to the hospital. She is not happy.

12:00: Back to the classroom to prepare for Math class. Teach a required 70-minute lesson.

1:10: Teach Science class and conduct the experiment for the second time.

1:55: Teach Science class and conduct the experiment for the third time. I have just enough materials this time.

2:40: Penmanship class and nobody is in the mood for it at this time of the day.

3:00: Homeroom Music class. I decide to focus on 80s music. Finally we are starting to wind down our day.

3:15: Get ready for dismissal.

3:30: A student misses his bus. I call home and arrange for the parents to pick him up. They are not happy.

3:40: Call back the parent from this morning. She is still not home, so I leave a message that we will make up the test together tomorrow morning.

3:45: Teachers are allowed to leave. I rush out the door to make it to day-care by the 4:00 dismissal time. I pick up my children and head home to make a quick dinner, and then head to the baseball fields where I will sit for the first time all day. Not quite yet—now they need a first base coach. Later that night, an hour of time is necessary to review homework assignments and do some planning for the next day of teaching.

There are thousands of stories that happen throughout a school year. This is just one of them.

TOM MONZO, JR., THIRD GRADE TEACHER

There are many Letters to the Editor espousing how easy teachers have it and how lucrative their jobs are. One such critic prompted a Pittsburgh area teacher to respond with the following letter that was published in the weekly paper:

Dr. Editor,

In response to [critic's name removed] Letter to the Editor, I would like to address his concerns. Where is your respect for the profession that helped make you who you are today? If teaching is such an attractive career, why don't you join us? [critic's name removed], please come over to the teaching sector where there is less money to be made compared to professions with similar educational requirements.

My guess is that you couldn't handle a career in teaching. Research shows a teacher engages in as many as 1,000 interpersonal exchanges during the course of a school day. This observation in itself testifies to the complexity and immediacy of the daily situation in which every teacher is forced to make decisions. Not surprisingly, effective teachers have been found to tolerate enormous amounts of ambiguity, uncertainty, unpredictability, and occasional chaos, as well as to be able to focus on the "here and now" of the physical and social realities of their classrooms.

Your argument about unions and tenure doesn't hold water either. The union can only protect a teacher to a certain extent. Tenure isn't what you think it is. Teachers are evaluated on a regular basis and are held accountable for their actions in- and outside the classroom. It's like living under a microscope at times.

Our production at [school district name withheld] is number one according to Standards and Poor's ratings. And how can you mention merit pay for teachers? We aren't on an assembly line where we can toss out a batch of parts that we have a problem with. I've worked in the private sector for merit pay and it is not a perfect system either.

Teachers often work past 3:30 PM. They also often work evening and summer jobs to compensate for the difference in pay when compared to other professions with similar educational backgrounds. While working supplemental jobs, teachers often encounter challenging interpersonal relationships with other workers. Often they are accused of double-dipping, while earning a below average hourly wage. I personally worked one summer from Memorial Day to Labor Day, six days a week, at two jobs, and began my day at 7 AM and ended at 9 PM. For all of that effort, I earned an extra $4,000. I gave up my vacation and still didn't catch up to other professionals with similar credentials.

How can private sector jobs be compared to teaching? You are not comparing apples to apples. There are too many variables in teaching, such as students' individual abilities, and extra teaching requirements, such as graduate school.

Lastly, you addressed the quality of teaching and how it won't be affected by underpaying our teachers. I'd like to return to my original argument. The teachers will continue to work above and beyond when they feel respected. Teaching is the profession that creates all other professions. In my opinion, there is no more important job in the world.

—Tom Monzo[5]

Personally knowing Mr. Monzo and having spent time in his school building and working with his fellow teachers in my staff development training programs, I can attest to the hard work and dedication that Tom and his colleagues do as teachers in today's schools.

TODAY'S REAL UNSUNG HEROES

Teachers are the real unsung heroes. All too often, we tend to look at professional athletes, rock musicians, and movie stars as heroes or role models when they are mere celebrities. Although many famous people have made important contributions to society and their communities, it is easy to overlook all of the good work that teachers do in today's school systems. Unfortunately, not much prominent news coverage is given to all of the heroes who are teaching today's children.

Everyday, teachers are making a difference. At any given moment in a typical school day, teachers are influencing children in positive and meaningful ways. So many problems exist, such as violence, drugs, broken homes, child abuse, economic crises, and a variety of other woes. We must acknowledge the fact that school systems today did NOT create these problems; we still have to deal with them every single day. The impact of society's turbulence is felt each day within the walls of our schools. It is the teachers who struggle with the turmoil of society while trying to offset the negative influences outside of school. Teachers are the real heroes, as they roll up their sleeves and take strides to improve the lives of their students.

A documentary presented a look at five new teachers as they experienced their first year of teaching. The production, entitled "The First Year," conveys the struggles and joy of teaching, as cameras followed the new teachers working with their students.

The article from the *Seattle Times*, dated April 24, 2002, states:

> The documentary was directed by Davis Guggenheim, who also has directed the feature film "Gossip" and television programs including "ER" and "NYPD Blue." Like many people, Davis Guggenheim started worrying about the state of public education when he became a parent.
>
> The more he read about the state of public schools, the more confused he became. But when he followed an acquaintance into the classroom one day, he decided teachers' stories were missing from the debate.
>
> "You see films that criticize the (school) system, and the politicians bat the thing around. It seemed to me that the effect that teachers were having was momentous, even though no one was seeing it."
>
> To change that, Guggenheim, the son of four-time Academy Award winner Charles Guggenheim, took cameras into five Los Angeles area classrooms. The result is a hymn to the passion and commitment of teachers everywhere who reach out to students when no one else does—principals, unreliable speech therapists, and their families.
>
> "I wanted it to be a simple message," Guggenheim says. "That there are passionate people out there who are making a huge difference, and we need to support these people, and find more of them."
>
> Guggenheim says he tried to make an apolitical film. His only agenda was to make people understand that "the job of a teacher is terribly hard and that the struggles are immense, but what they're doing is so heroic and, in the end, so fulfilling."

"In many ways, the film is a sort of Rorschach card," he says. "People draw a lot of conclusions that I never intended. But it's impossible to see this film and not say that a teacher with a sense of purpose can make a huge difference and we need more of them and we need to support them once they're there."

He says he fell in love with all teachers and admired what they do.[6]

It is very refreshing to see a movie director become an advocate of teachers and show admiration for the work that they do. The efforts of Davis Guggenheim should be saluted. We are in need of more examples like this that portray the realities of teaching.

2

THE ATTRIBUTES OF A TEACHER

Certain characteristics have been associated with good teaching. Effective teachers are said to have a gift of patience, subject matter expertise, a desire to make a difference, and a caring attitude.

In my direct work with teachers, classroom discussion has often focused on what makes a great teacher. Teachers have identified their qualities as:

- personal magnetism and optimism
- enthusiasm and passion
- creative and effective planners
- professional attitude and accessibility
- class control and responsiveness
- communication skills
- being able to relate to students
- understanding of students needs
- expertise in one's subject

Many of these traits have focused more on personality factors and less on knowledge or teaching strategies.

In this era of educational reform, there seems to be more of a shift toward judging a teacher's effectiveness by such qualities as: (1) proper monitoring of learning activities, (2) demonstrated classroom skills, (3) testing and grading, (4) subject matter knowledge, and (5) skills related to how well teachers know and understand how to perform their duties. There is more of a focus on student standardized test scores and how they represent teacher effectiveness. This course of action has led to increased pressures and demands on today's teacher.

In spite of the focus on data-driven assessment, there still exists the type of teacher who is memorable. We all remember those special teachers who taught with passion, had a desire to impart their knowledge to us, were caring and considerate, and truly loved teaching. Those memories may have even affected our decision to pursue teaching as a profession.

I often invite teachers to participate in a little activity entitled "Three Questions." In this activity, teachers are asked to reflect upon their experiences as a second grade student and to reminisce on that special time when they were very young and impressionable. I then ask them a few questions:

"By a show of hands, how many of you remember who the governor of your state was while you were in second grade?" I have yet to see any hands go up.

Then I ask, "By a show of hands, how many remember who the President of the United States was?" Usually, two or three hands are raised. I then ask the question, "By a show of hands, who remembers the name of their second grade teacher?" Suddenly all hands are raised, and most of their faces are smiling. Fond and positive memories are associated with these recollections of their second grade teachers. I take it a step further and ask them to identify their most memorable teacher and explain why they picked that person. This always leads to a lively discussion. In their small group discussions, comments and examples are most often positive and always include an expression of gratitude for the influence that special teacher has made in their own lives.

Today's teacher is more than a transmitter of knowledge; the demands of our profession are ever increasing. Many parents have an expectation that the school system should be the "do all and be all" in their children's lives. Parents have a notion that they can drop off their child at the school house door, and behold, twelve years later, they will be able to pick-up a perfect specimen of a human being—well-rounded, academically proficient, emotionally sound, physically fit, and ready to meet the next phase of life. But we know that teachers cannot do it alone. Parental involvement that results in a partnership in the child's development is necessary.

Think of all of the roles, duties, and titles that are placed on you as a teacher. You are wearing many hats—today's teacher is a coach, mentor, counselor, advisor, listener, nutritionist, bookkeeper, entertainer, and, yes, a teacher, too.

A PASSION FOR TEACHING

I did not go into teaching to strike it rich, financially, that is. We do know, however, that teachers achieve richness in other areas of their lives. We fully realize that the richness comes in the form of personal satisfaction, academic progress, and other personal goals. For example, we have a certain amount of control over how we teach the curriculum. The profession certainly allows for a great amount of creativity. Ultimately, we directly influence the future of our community. And we *do* get those summer vacations. But teaching, like no other profession, offers a great degree of personal satisfaction to those who truly have a passion for teaching.

One of my favorite movies is *Flashdance* (1983). This hit film was shot primarily in Pittsburgh, Pennsylvania. Having lived there for most of my adult life, I immediately became a fan of the movie and its upbeat soundtrack. More recently, I have rediscovered that wonderful music.

The award-winning soundtrack spawned several top-forty hits in the 1980s, including the title song, "Flashdance," by Irene Cara. I think it still offers us a significant motivational theme. What a Feeling! It is a special feeling, even though we don't always choose to admit it. It is that inspirational feeling that keeps us entering the classroom year after year. Cara sings, "Take your passion and make it happen." I believe it is your passion that makes it happen. Your passion for the subject, the students, and the journey is what drives you to succeed.

WHY DID YOU BECOME A TEACHER?

Some questions for your consideration: Of all the 20,000 or so job titles and occupations that are listed in the Department of Labor's *Dictionary* of *Occupational Titles* (DOT), why did you select teaching as your chosen profession? Why did you bypass all of the other twenty-some-thousand jobs and focus on a career in teaching? What prompted you to become a teacher? Take some time to reflect on your answers. Put the book aside for a while and concentrate on where you were when you made the decision to pursue a teaching career. This is in important exercise because often we may lose sight on what motivated us to want to teach in the first place.

In your mind's eye, picture yourself as if you were in a movie—you're watching yourself. What are you doing? Who are you with? Or are you alone? Are you in school, on a playground, in church, in the woods? What circumstances in your life at that time prompted this decision? Now that you have recollected and visualized it, please write your reasons below:

Why did you become a teacher?

_____

_____

_____

_____

_____

When did you first decide to become a teacher and what influenced you?

_____

_____

_____

_____

_____

Take more time to reflect if you have to. Close the book and really try to rekindle the true passion that prompted your decision. Reach back and re-discover that inspiration. Think about your responses and add to your reflections in your journal—you *do* keep a journal, don't you?

LIGHT THE FLAME WITHIN

I have always been a big fan of the Olympics. The competition level is always impressive as the world's best athletes gather to perform. In addition to the actual performance in direct competition, there is a tremendous amount of preparation, practice, and dedication done prior to the actual events. Olympic athletes devote thousands of hours of time behind the scenes performing and practicing their respective sports over and over again. These athletes commit themselves to all of the necessary conditioning, drills, preparation, and perseverance necessary to compete at their best levels possible.

Teaching is very much like an Olympic competition. Just think of all the hours and hours of planning time that you do. You know of the additional time it takes to prepare a lesson, as well as the time after teaching in terms of assessment, evaluation, and student feedback. In your classroom, you are on the playing field. In the same way that an Olympic athlete devotes thousands of hours in practice and preparation, so do you as a teacher.

Another part of the Olympics that interests me is the inspiring "Olympic Torch Relay." The running of the torch from Atlanta, Georgia, to Salt Lake City, Utah, to "light the flame" is an amazing event. I had the opportunity to witness the torch relay as it progressed through my own town. On January 1, 2002, I watched the flame as it was carried through Erie, Pennsylvania, on its way to Salt Lake City. As the caravan motored its way across the country, spectators and residents cheered as it passed. I was impressed to see that one of the torchbearers in Erie was an 88-year-old woman who overcame adversity and bounced back to live an active life. Another woman, Sarah McClelland, carried the torch on to Morraine, Ohio, and became the Winter Games' oldest torchbearer, at the age of 102. By the time the eternal flame arrived in Utah, it had traveled more than 13,500 miles through 46 states, and it passed through the hands of more than 11,500 torchbearers.

Keep that in mind next time you may need to be inspired. A reminder of their accomplishments could give you that needed boost of energy to make it through your next difficult day. Check out the appendix in the back of this book. There are many quotes and thoughts that will inspire you.

The 2002 Olympic slogan, "Light the Fire Within," and the 2006 slogan, "Passion Lives Here," both have special significance to me. Teachers have always had the unique ability to light the flame and keep the fire of learning burning with desire within their students. Passion does live within each one of them, and they ignite that passion within the hearts of their students.

This is evident in their classrooms and their interactions with students day to day. In many respects that is what teaching is all about. In your daily toils, endeavors, and woes, you are truly lighting the flame of learning. You are passing the torch of learning and the love of learning to your students on a daily basis. This transference is a powerful process. You are influencing the future as you transmit the knowledge, skills, and traits that your students need to compete in the real world.

Think of what you've done that enables you to teach and has given you the right to teach. Just like an athlete, you prepared for four years (or more) as an undergraduate, course after course, until that day you graduate. Getting that degree was like developing an expertise in an Olympic sport or event. Only later did you begin the right of passage, enabling you to teach with the confidence of a world-class athlete.

A teacher's work is never done. Once you begin teaching, you then need to continue your own education. Your role as a lifelong learner is never done. Just like that skilled athlete, you are constantly updating your education, perhaps earning a graduate degree or two, and also making sure your teaching certificate is active and valid.

You are very much like that Olympic athlete. Your next lesson is your next level of competition. Your classroom is your arena, the four walls of your room is the stadium, and the coliseum is where you perform and compete. You are on display, you are performing, and you are being judged by your students, their parents, your building principal, as well as politicians, taxpayers, political watch dogs, the public, the media, the school board, and your fellow educators.

Through your role as a teacher, you are inspiring your students to live up to their potentials. You are preparing them for their own tomorrows. When they gradate from your school systems, they then have "the torch" to take with them for their next journey, the next generation.

3

CLASSROOM SUCCESS

When working with groups of teachers over the years, either on staff development days or in graduate education courses, I often began a class session with the following brainteaser: What are the six Ps of classroom success? The answer?

Prior **P**reparation and **P**lanning **P**revents **P**oor **P**erformance

The key to success in the classroom deals with deliberate planning, thorough preparation, and being ready to perform. The six Ps are an important axiom for any educator, a first-year teacher or a veteran of 30+ years. Planning and preparation separate the teaching profession from most other professions. Granted, other professions have their share of planning, but teaching is unique because the process of planning never ends.

Planning is one aspect that is not fully understood by today's critics. These critics often look at a school schedule of starting times versus dismissal times and make the unfair assumption that a teacher's day is very short and not very demanding.

I remember once as I walked down the hall of a community college on the way to a meeting, a sign on a faculty member's door caught my eye. I had to stop and read the sign over again. It said: "When a teacher is reading a book, she is working."

I am sure that the statement was meant for the administration members who had offices nearby, but for the majority of the public, the image of a teacher quietly reading probably conjures up the notion of someone slacking off. After all, reading for most people is a leisure activity, not part of the job. Teachers, however, have been in the information business long before computer networks and the Internet. Reading is an essential part of the planning and preparation process.

So, how does a teacher deal better with all of the time constraints? Another important notion is what I call the "168 Factor." This, too, has been a popular brainteaser in my work with fellow educators.

What does 168 represent?

You've probably guessed that the number 168 represents time. In any given week, there are exactly 168 hours—7 days a week times 24 hours per day. The important realization occurs when one understands that "that's all there is, folks." No more, no less. Time is something we can't save, store, or make more of. We have to use it and it is there for our disposal—168 hours to do all we have to do in a one-week time frame.

No wonder we are so tired. So what's the solution? Priority planning is the key. It's important to get into the daily habit of prioritizing our time. A common approach to deciding what is important versus what is not important is to ask the following question:

What is the most productive use of my time right now?

For teachers, issues of time are more vital than with other professions. You are constantly aware of time considerations: length of class periods, time on task, individual lessons, units, semesters, block scheduling, and so on. Whether you are departmentalized or self-contained within your subject matter and content areas, time is an important consideration. Being cognizant of time constraints is always a priority and multitasking is essential.

As a social studies teacher, I saw my days get busier and busier. I found my reading time becoming severely limited. In addition to reading, I also enjoy exercising with some form of vigorous physical fitness activity each day. So, rather than doing just one at a time, I combine or stack them. It is very common for me to be exercising on a stationary bicycle and reading at the same time. While using the stair-master machine, I also read newspapers, professional journals, and other pertinent publications. An alternative is to tune the T.V. to an all-news channel and watch while working out.

In order to have something with me all the time, I always carry a reading file containing articles, journal clippings, correspondence, book reviews, and other materials. Having this file handy has helped me in many other situations, such as waiting at a doctor's appointment, during car maintenance, or when I arrive early for a meeting.

Recently I went to one of those "10-minute oil change" establishments and found that the 10 minutes actually turned into a 40-minute wait. I noticed that some other customers were upset, pacing the floor and stewing about the extended wait, whereas I welcomed the extra time to devote to my reading file. In addition, I had a chance to review my planning calendar and do some extra mental preparation for my next speaking presentation. My point is this: although I had planned for a ten-minute oil change, the unexpected wait was turned into a productive mini-work session.

Years ago on a college campus photocopy center door, I saw a large sign that read: "Poor planning on *your* part, does NOT make an emergency on *my* part." Whenever a fellow professor was in need of a rush job on some photocopying, the print room attendant merely pointed to the sign as a way of politely informing the unorganized person that others were ahead of him and that he would just have to wait his turn. That's an important reminder for all of us: plan ahead to avoid the last-minute rush job and you will be further ahead and more organized as a result.

SELF-TALK: POSITIVE WORD USAGE AND AFFIRMATIONS

"I feel happy, I feel healthy, I feel terrific!"
"Today is going to be a great day—make it happen!"
"I think I can, I think I can . . . I know I can . . . I will."

The process of self-talk holds tremendous power. We constantly carry on a silent conversation with ourselves. Many of our thoughts, however, are negative and contain self-defeating attitudes. As educators, we know all to well that words can be extremely powerful.

The very words we choose, whether through self-talk, in conversations with others, or in the classroom can set the stage for either a positive or negative experience. Here is a good example. Over the years, I have often begun my class sessions or presentations with the following affirmative statement: "I anticipate a successful day of learning for all of us." By beginning with such a positive statement, it sets up anticipation in the class or the audience that they are going to have a positive experience. "Let's make today a success," fixes the idea of accomplishment in the minds of the participants.

Positive self-talk tends to lead to positive results; whereas negative thinking tends to lead to negative results. Remember the old adage of a glass that is filled halfway? The positive, optimistic person views it as "half-full," while the negative, pessimistic individual sees it as "half-empty." This type of outlook tends to carry over into everyday life as well. Positive individuals are on the "look-out" for the good in all endeavors. Coupled with positive expectations, maintaining an optimistic attitude often leads to greater results in life.

A better way to manage our attitudes is through the use of affirmations. We can actually choose words that create positive messages to ourselves. Through conscious repetition, such phrases as "act enthusiastic and you will become enthusiastic" can actually help you find more energy and you will naturally become more upbeat. The use of positive affirmations greatly increases the likelihood that something good will actually happen; we open ourselves up to the possibility that these opportunities exist. Affirmations and positive self-talk are also ways of maintaining an optimistic outlook on either a particular situation or life in general.

When I get up in the morning, I begin the day by saying, "I am full of energy, vitality, strength, and enthusiasm!" Now before you laugh too hard, I will admit that I initially do not feel that way. Yet, what I have found is that by saying it over and over again, I actually begin to feel that way. On the contrary, if I were to chose to begin each day by saying, "Oh, no, morning already? I'm so tired. I need more sleep," then that is exactly how I would feel. I would go about my morning routine being tired, sleepy, and ready for nothing.

I am reminded of a television commercial for an instant breakfast drink. A man sits on the edge of the bed drinking from the can. He says things like, "Work is good." By the end of the sixty-second spot, he puts on the head of a chicken costume and is rearing to go. The moral is this: a positive attitude can make any job a positive experience. Try this just once—make it a point to begin your day differently. When the alarm clock rings and you stretch and rub your eyes, say—yes, say it out loud— a positive affirmation like, "I am full of energy, vitality, strength, and enthusiasm!" It just might work.

Now, apply the same strategy to your own classroom. Do you hear students saying, "Oh, no, time for math," or making comments like, "I'm never going to get this," "I hate this subject," or "This is too difficult"? If so, then you may want to try using the positive approach with affirmations that accentuate the spirit of optimism.

A person I know—I'll call him Ozzie—introduced me to a very powerful way of looking at each day with positive expectations. Ozzie would always share this bit of advice with everyone he met: "Start each day with positive and eager anticipation, and end each night with pleasant memories."

Remember that last lousy lesson that you had? Chances are that you may have expected it. And what about the lesson that went very well for you? You probably anticipated that it would go well for you. Next time, try giving yourself an internal "pep talk" that says things will go well and that your next lesson will be a success. In addition to your self-talk, think about how it will sound in the classroom. At the start of a lesson, do you find yourself saying, "This will be difficult" or "This next concept is very complex"? In other words, be careful of how you begin presenting new information and especially avoid labels that would tend to set up negative expectations or foster negative anticipation about the subject. Of course, words alone will not magically lead to success. We need to constantly remind our students about the importance of hard work, perseverance, determination, and "stickability," that is, sticking with something until it is fully understood.

Nevertheless, when dealing with our students or maintaining a dialog within ourselves, the importance of maintaining a positive outlook cannot be overemphasized. Too many of our students come from homes that do not focus on the positive. Do you ever listen to parents talk to their children in public? Do you hear things like, "Don't do that! You're bad!" or "You'll never amount to anything!"? If anything, we need to use positive wording just to try to counteract the negative phrasing that is all too familiar.

In addition to positive self-talk and affirmations, another consideration is the power of positive word usage. Just think of how often we tell our students "what not to do" instead of "what to do." For instance, we may commonly try to remind a forgetful student to act responsibly.

You say, "Johnny, don't forget to bring your math book tomorrow." A more effective approach would be to say, "Johnny, remember to bring your math book tomorrow."

Here's another example. Consider this announcement: "Don't Panic!" What on earth does that mean? Writer Douglas Adams features this satirical comment in the classic *The Hitchhiker's Guide to the Galaxy* series. Just the mention of something that suggests a crisis causes most people to expect the worst. Conversely, at crucial times when calm is important, it is better to announce, "Remain Calm." Positive wording is very powerful.

During a recent baseball game while the pitcher was beginning to waver, the coach jogged out to the mound and gave the pitcher what he thought was some good, solid advice. Face to face with the nervous pitcher, during a close, crucial game, and about to face the opponent's best hitter, the coach said, "Whatever you do, don't give him a high, outside pitch; he will knock it out of the park."

The coach was feeling pretty good with himself as he strode back to the dugout. Through careful study and meticulous analysis, the coach realized the tendencies of this hitter and the strengths of his batting style. The coach sat down, ready for the next play, and the pitcher paused a moment and then threw a hard, fast pitch "high and outside." The crack of the bat thundered throughout the stadium. It happened just as the coach had predicted: high and outside = a home run. Had that coach known the importance of positive wording, he would have given the pitcher the following instructions: "Whatever you do, be sure to give him a low, inside pitch, so you will strike him out."

Not far from where I live is a restaurant near a very busy intersection. There is a sign that reads, "Keep this driveway entrance open," instead of a traditional sign that would have read, "Do Not Block This Entrance." Think about it. The emphasis is on open rather than Do Not Block. I have always noticed a greater degree of cooperation with the message that is positively phrased. It is almost as if the positively phrased statement invites the reader to be an active participant in the situation. When empowered in this manner, people will inevitably take part in the process and cooperate with the positive message. These real examples depict a powerful way to get students, athletes, and others to cooperate, to be more effective, and to be more willing to follow your instructions.

SELF-TALK FOR A MORE SUCCESSFUL YEAR OR 180 DAYS AND COUNTING

If your state defines its school year as 180 days, which is very common, you may want to view that time frame as a marathon. A marathon requires your utmost attention, grueling preparation, superhuman endurance, endless stamina, and a host of other qualities that make long-distance runners unique in the sports world. As you run your own marathon through the school year, you must draw on all your talents and abilities, dig up new reserves of energy, and end your race in a successful fashion. This one-day-at-a-time philosophy can be one effective way to approach the typical school year.

Your own positive self-talk makes a big difference as you approach the beginning of a school year, and an essential addition as you are in the midst of it. The words we choose to describe something can either make or break a situation or circumstance. To avoid becoming overwhelmed, look at each day as a new beginning. Try to view each day as the *first day of the rest of the school year*.

This first-day attitude is one great way to cope with all the unavoidable difficulties. If one day suddenly becomes a miserable day for you, then reflect on it, learn from it, and move on. After all, tomorrow is a chance to recover and reestablish the momentum you need to make it through the entire academic year.

That next-day attitude can also foster a spirit of competition. Often in athletic events, when the outcome is not what was expected or desired, there is always that next match or race. Take on that "wait until next time" perspective. As you start each day and you return to your classroom each morning, get ready, get set, and GO! As you bounce back from the day before, keep your chin up, and never, never give up.

Inspirational writer Reverend Bob Schuller often tells his congregations and audiences, "Inch by inch, it's a cinch; by the yard, it's hard." If you maintain that inch-by-inch type of attitude, you can make great strides. If you go for the incremental, bit-by-bit approach to sticking with it, you can finish the marathon and still retain your sanity, maintain your energy levels, and begin your vacation time with the same enthusiasm you are used to.

Start to look at the entire school year as a series of manageable time frames that you can conquer one at a time. A walk is completed step by step. A wall is built stone by stone. Each day can be a new ball game, each classroom a new arena, each problem another opponent for you to outscore, pass on the outside, pin to the mat.

The determination and persistence of your efforts is guaranteed to pay off. Regroup, reorganize, and rest when you must, but do not quit. It's always easy to give in and say, "Oh, well, it looks like it's going to be just one of those days." But it is just as easy to make that same day "one of those days" when things improve, things get better, and you begin to make important inroads with your students. All of a sudden your lessons become more effective. Your students' test scores do improve. And you are the reason. Completion of the entire school year involves this continuous incremental approach. View each day as another chance to make inroads to your students' achievement levels.

Here is a story involving four letters: T, H, I, and O. One person, who was positive, enthusiastic, and optimistic, would begin each day with a "THIO" perspective. Upon talking with another person for a while, he would then ask what that person thought the four letters stood for, just so he could then compare frames of mind. Most often, the response was negative and very different from how he defined the four letters. For instance, one typical response he received was "The Heat Is On," another "The Honeymoon Is Over" and occasionally with some reversed the letters, "Only I Have Troubles." He found these negative responses amusing. He then became even more convinced that his interpretation of the four-letter outlook was right on target. You see, this person chose "Today Has Its Opportunities" as his outlook on life.

I always try to find snippets of wisdom to share with others. A well-worded quote or some positive aphorism can go a long way in bringing home a point that I'm trying to make—especially about the teaching profession. The following is my own "Words to Live By," my creed, if you will:

The Effective Teacher's Creed

I am a teacher of tremendous talent and capability. I possess unlimited human potential.

I can accomplish whatever my thoughts can create and that in which I believe.

My knowledge, experience, and training enable me to teach my students effectively.

Through prior proper planning and lesson design, I can help my students accomplish great things.

In my mind's eye, I will always see myself as a successful teacher.

Through visualization and mental rehearsal, I can be ready to teach my next great lesson.

I see myself and my teaching career and what lies ahead of me with a new dimension.

With a renewed spirit of optimism, I will begin to transfer these ideas and thoughts into action.

My actions will then generate new feelings of passion toward my teaching.

I will feel the way I think and I will act in a positive and renewed fashion.

Through this approach, and by always being prepared, I will then experience greater success, happiness, and personal satisfaction for a job well-done.

This inner peace and contentment will lead toward teaching with more energy, love, belief, passion, and a sense of satisfaction in what I do in the classroom.

As I teach my next lesson, I will act in an enthused manner!

I will act out in a positive sense toward my belief in myself as a teacher, my curriculum, my school, and my colleagues with whom I teach!

I will be a teacher who acts rather than reacts to change.

I will always be a teacher of action.

I know that I can make things happen.

I know that if it's meant to be, then, it's up to me!

I will maintain my drive, ambition, determination, persistence, and endurance.

I will make things happen!

I will take my passion for teaching and make good things happen.

> *For I am a master teacher, and will work wonders with my students!*
> *I will take my passion and make it happen!*

Tom Staszewski, 2007

This teacher's creed is designed to lift your spirits and reinvigorate your passion for teaching. The next time you begin to doubt your effectiveness as a teacher, read it out loud to yourself. Try it in a mirror so you can see yourself and hear the words. Read it periodically just to remind yourself of the abilities you have and all of the years of preparation that it took to enable you to teach. The creed can be a means of reinforcing your inner spirit and a renewal to reinvigorate your passion for teaching. Use my creed as a springboard to compose your own as well. You can add your specific, unique talents and inspire yourself. Post it prominently so others can see it. You might just inspire others, too.

The more we choose to think positive, to focus on the good, and to look at what's right with life, rather than what's wrong, the better off we will be. Let's face it. We do have a choice to be either positive or negative in our thinking. Granted, we can also choose to be more of middle-of-the-road or neutral in our thought process, yet, for the most part, it is either a positive or negative pattern that we develop and maintain.

The human mind has often been compared to a computer or even a garden. If we put in positive, optimistic thoughts for the input, we then process that which is positive and the end result or output is likely to also be positive. The same holds true for the GIGO approach: Garbage In leads to Garbage Out. Think about it; the disk or data that we enter into our minds tends to have an influence on our outcomes in life.

Here are some suggestions to get you started on the path to a more positive, optimistic choice and, thus, a more harmonious and enthusiastic mind-set and end result of your efforts:

1. Always have something to look forward to! Seeing a loved one, participating in a hobby you enjoy, or taking that all-important vacation or weekend getaway—something to build up a desire within you of positive anticipation.
2. Life is too short as it is! The more you realize that you can't control *everything* and that time tends to pass us by, the more you can enjoy yourself. Now is the time to appreciate the fact that life can

pass us by while we are grouchy or irritable. Don't get caught in the trap of negative thinking and let life pass you by. Get busy, enjoy the moment.

3. Some people have it worse than you do. Appreciate what you have and enjoy who you are. You may have a feeling that you are in a difficult situation, but work through it, keep your chin up, and look for some good to come out of the hardship.

4. Put it in perspective. Look at the big picture of life. If you look at the bigger picture of your situation, chances are you will see, in reality, that it is probably pretty insignificant. I'm not dismissing your hardships and difficulties, merely asking you to put it into perspective, or to ask yourself what is the worst thing that could possibly happen. Oftentimes, this kind of an assessment can help you to better cope with life's struggles and to maintain hope for either a better day or for a resolution to what's bothering you.

5. Take a break and come back refreshed! If you find that steps 1–4 have not helped you, then maybe you need a quick getaway—a walk around the block, a short drive in your car, moving to another location in your home, or going for an ice-cream cone. Sometimes a change of pace or a different venue can work magic on our dispositions.

Remember that attitude is everything. What we think about can literally make or break the situation. Through your attitude, you filter all of your experiences and everything that happens to you. Your attitude leads to how you view yourself and your set of circumstances.

HOW TO BE MORE ENERGETIC AND ENTHUSIASTIC

Years ago, as a student in the world-famous "Dale Carnegie Course," I remember a session on enthusiasm. The instructor led us through some cheers that focused on becoming more enthusiastic. The instructor asked us to say over and over again, with meaning, conviction, and energy, "act enthusiastic and you will be enthusiastic." As we continued to say it, an amazing thing started to happen; we actually began to generate enthusiasm. The level of enthusiasm in the meeting room increased.

To become more enthusiastic, it is important to act enthusiastic. To gain an increased level of enthusiasm and energy, we need to choose words that are conducive to our feelings. To offset that negative feeling, say to yourself: "Act enthusiastic and I will be enthusiastic" and other such positive statements such as, "I am energetic" or "I am full of energy, vitality, and strength."

Students appreciate teachers who are animated, enthusiastic, and energetic. For a moment think about yourself as a student. Didn't you appreciate and value more a teacher who was full of energy, over one who was drab, listless, or dull? What about those memorable teachers that you recall to this day? Aren't those who are most vivid in your mind, those who stand out above the rest; didn't they have the most energy and taught with a high level of enthusiasm?

While watching T.V. recently, I saw a speaker who was excited. His arms were gesturing wildly, his eyes were alive with emotion as he spoke, and he was animated with an upbeat inflection in the tone of his voice. He definitely captured my attention; I found him to be enthralling and entertaining. I soon became convinced that I needed to listen to him even more. I learned a lot about his particular topic and liked his entertaining, enthusiastic, and energetic approach to speaking. What made this speaker so captivating and convincing? It was his energy! He was incredibly dynamic and inspiring, and I was motivated to keep listening.

How does one go about acquiring the necessary energy and stamina to become more captivating and to be better able to enthrall a classroom? In my own situation as a speaker, trainer, and consultant, I know of the importance of being energetic during my presentations.

A major part of planning and preparation for my presentations now consists of creating within myself higher levels of energy, so that I will come across in a more energized fashion. The next time you have a need to increase your synergy and to become livelier, give the following suggestions a try:

1. Realize the importance of teaching with energy. The more you convince yourself that it is important to teach with a heightened sense of enthusiasm, the more you can sustain it. When you are energetic, people will want to be around you, your students will be more receptive to your ideas, and your class will be more likely to "buy into" what you are saying.

2. Follow your passion. Passion brought you into the teaching profession. Now your goal is to develop even more passion so that you can persevere and sustain the necessary amount of vitality to teach more effectively.

3. Animate yourself. Movement, gestures, and body language can be magical. The best educators realize that students are more attentive to an animated teacher. You only need to watch young children as they naturally demonstrate their surprise, wonderment, and amazement at things that they find or experience.

4. Energize with laughter.

5. Realize that acting is a part of teaching. Probably within each teacher is an actor in disguise. Both teachers and actors need to first capture, hold, and then captivate an audience. In the classroom, on the silver screen, or in the theater, it is important to project an image, stay focused, and effectively deliver the message or portray a character effectively to the audience. A lot of this involves a script of self-talk, mental rehearsal, visualizing, and repetition to better fix the characteristics of the energetic character within you. You can then assume the role that you will be "playing" in your classroom.

6. Maintain a consistent sleep schedule. An inconsistent sleep schedule can sap your natural energy flow and lead to more sluggish days.

7. Drink plenty of water. Dehydration can rapidly zap your energy level and make you more sluggish. Stay hydrated and you will feel better; plus, water is beneficial for maintaining your vocal cords.

These seven tips can assist you in keeping your energy levels and enthusiasm high and combat fatigue, depression, and sluggishness. If you make it a point to follow the above suggestions, you can become more lively and active in your personal life and be better able to meet the challenges of the teaching profession.

OVERCOMING THE URGE TO PROCRASTINATE

The hardest part of any job is getting started.

—J. C. Penney

Determine in what areas you may have a tendency to procrastinate. Assess just where you are most prone to procrastinate. For instance, ask yourself if you tend to put off grading exams, filing papers, answering letters, or returning phone calls. Perhaps one or some of those may be what you tend to avoid. If so, then being aware of what you don't want to do—when you should be doing it instead—is an important realization for you. Once you have pinpointed those areas that you tend to delay, make a concentrated area to develop more of a sense of urgency and convince yourself of the importance of getting started and accomplishing what needs to be done. Here are some specific steps to help you conquer procrastination:

1. Divide and conquer. Break the project into smaller, more manageable parts. Busy teachers seldom have the luxury of large chunks of time. Taking 20 minutes of time here and there is more realistic than having a total three hours available to do nothing else but work on that project.
2. Establish a deadline. Set a timetable up front as to when you need to be done with the task. Forecasting a deadline date or submission time and appropriately marking your planning calendar to remind yourself of the due date is essential.
3. Do the most important things first. Procrastinators tend to do trivial and routine tasks as a means of looking busy while there are more high-priority items that really need to be done.
4. Strive for excellence, not perfection. Perfectionism can be counterproductive. Be more realistic of what you can and can't do, and always do your best, be your best, and know that nothing is ever perfect.
5. Reward yourself for your accomplishments. For example, free up some time to work on that important matter, and then once you've finalized it, be kind to yourself. Recognize your efforts by doing something you enjoy. An occasional treat can help you to develop a greater sense of momentum, and it can sustain your efforts to stick with something until it is done.
6. Discipline yourself to use your planning time wisely. Make it a point to devote all of your planning time on the specific task that you need to complete that day. What about that time before and after school? Perhaps you can make more efficient use of those time frames.

7. Remember that procrastination is just like a mirage based on a false premise. It disguises and distorts itself in the everyday routine and mundane tasks so that we get bogged down, and we know full well that our attention should be elsewhere. Procrastination has a way of sneaking up on you and can rob you of your peace of mind. We think we have all the time in the world ahead of us; yet, in actuality, we don't.

LEARNING HOW TO SAY "NO" (AND FEEL GOOD ABOUT IT)

A common cause of not having enough time may be due to your tendency to say "yes" when you really mean "no." If you find yourself taking on too many tasks, are overobligated, or agreeing to mounting requests, then perhaps you may need some help in saying NO. Teachers, by the nature of our profession, naturally feel an obligation to want to help. If you extended yourself and are constantly running behind on deadlines and due dates, then you probably have taken on too much.

As we look at the importance of *learning how to say "NO,"* let me stress that I am not referring to turning down those requests that are a part of our teaching positions. Nor am I recommending that you tell your building principal, "No, I'm not going to do that"; what I am addressing is being comfortable in turning down those requests that are not really a part of your job duties and responsibilities.

When appropriately used, learning to say "no" can be one of your most effective means of saving time. All too often, failure to say "no" can result in you doing the priorities of other people, rather than your own. This is not a selfish or self-centered approach; it merely suggests that you carefully weigh those requests that you know you really shouldn't be doing.

We have many reasons why most people find it difficult to say no to friends or even casual acquaintances. For instance, you may have a fear of offending someone else. You may have a desire to win someone's approval, or there may be some humanitarian desire that you have to want to help others. In addition, a false sense of obligation, timidity, or worry of some sort of retaliation might lead you to say yes instead of no.

It's very easy to say yes to requests and then end up regretting it. If you are one to quickly agree to do things that you really do not have the time to take on, then be sure to ask some questions before you answer. Be sure to assess the consequences of your decision and weigh what the expectations are for your involvement. I have found that first questioning the other person as to the particulars, such as the amount of work involved or what the target date of completion is, can give me more of a realistic view of what the request entails.

If you fail to say no when you should, then you need to better recognize the trade-off that you are making. If you spread yourself too thin, it can lead to health problems and adverse stress, and ultimately decrease your efficiency. The quality of your performance can start to wane; thus, it is often better to do less very well than take on more and do it poorly.

The best reason to say no is to stick with the commitment you have for your own priorities. If you don't have your own specific priorities, then it is easy for others to determine your priorities. Be certain to give yourself some time to consider the request. Ask for more information on what is expected and count to ten before responding. Perhaps you can help in other ways without saying yes. Or maybe you can agree to get involved in a more limited capacity. Know ahead of time what kinds of things you won't do, are not your responsibilities, or are counterproductive. Say "no" with meaning and be consistent. Don't worry about losing any popularity. Just know your limits.

If you say yes to something new, ideally, it can be connected to at least not having to do an old one. This kind of trade-off can help you to better "weed out" those past obligations that may be getting in the way of your efficiency. This is an important step. If a new "yes" is taken on, then remember to balance it out by eliminating something else. You need to subtract an obligation to better balance out that new addition. However, what usually happens is by saying yes, you've merely added an additional item to your "things-to-do list." Remember, you know both addition and subtraction, so use both accordingly.

At all times, remember that you cannot achieve your priorities unless you learn how to more effectively decline, in a tactful and firm way, requests that do not contribute to the accomplishment of your goals and aspirations. Be realistic with what you can and can't do; there are only so many hours in a day, and those 24 hours can only go so far.

If you say no to a request and then are badgered by the requester to reconsider or made to feel guilty, then be firm by using the following types of statements:

1. "No, I cannot accept your request, as it is not a part of my goal structure right now."
2. "What part of no don't you understand? (in a neutral tone and avoid sarcasm)"
3. "No is a complete and full sentence!"

It's not up to you to do everything. As you get more comfortable with saying no, remember to maintain a firm stand and to stick with your decision to decline taking on another obligation.

If you are still not convinced that you can cut back and be more selective by saying no when you should, then keep these ideas in mind, as well:

1. Just because you are presently working on an annual project or event doesn't mean you are stuck with it year, after year, after year. Set a term limit or a transition year to phase out your involvement and stick with it.
2. Be very selective about which new (if any) group, organization, association, or committee you join. Make an agreement ahead of time with yourself. Determine the number you can manage and not overextend yourself.
3. Avoid changing your personal plans just because someone else asks you to do a chore. Simply state that you already have plans, even if your plan is to do nothing. The "down-time" can be advantageous.

Keep your planning calendar with you at all times. You will then be able to quickly refer to it and determine on the spot if you are available to do something. Your calendar can give you a better assessment of prior obligations and commitments. Keep in mind, too, that just because you see some open spaces on your calendar, doesn't necessarily mean that you are available to take on more responsibilities. Set aside some time for yourself.

4

MOTIVATION

What motivates you? What prompts you to move? What is your source of motivation? Can you motivate others? People do things for many different reasons—their reasons, not yours, and of course, students do things for their own reasons. In some cases, the motivation is just an acquired habit, some pattern of behavior that worked in the past and continues in the present.

I feel that motivation can be summarized in five words: What's In It for Me. Motivation is based on wants and needs.

Abraham Maslow's classic definition of a hierarchy of needs further substantiates this importance. You probably remember Maslow's pyramid[7] from a psychology class (see figure 4.1).

Well, because Maslow proposed that we are motivated intrinsically by our needs, what role do our wants have? In what ways do the things we want differ from what we need?

> I can accept failure. Everyone fails at something.
> But I can't accept not trying.
> It doesn't matter if you win as long as you
> give everything in your heart.
>
> —Michael Jordan

Figure 4.1.   Maslow's hierarchy of needs.[7]

While in high school, Michael Jordan's talent was not evident and he didn't make the basketball team. What if he accepted the assessment that he had no talent? What if he was not motivated to go back the next year? Well, for his own good, he didn't stop trying and that enabled the millions of his fans and supporters to enjoy his special talent and unique personality. Thank goodness he believed enough in himself to keep trying.

GOAL SETTING

Have you ever heard the old saying, "I'm waiting for my ship to come in"? I believe there are many people, even professionals among us, who are indeed "waiting for their ship to come in," and I'm convinced that they will wait and wait, with no ship sightings and no results. I've always said that in order for that ship to come in, one must first send one out. The law of reciprocity applies here. If we truly want our ship to come in so we can reap all of the rewards, benefits, and payoffs, then we must first make the effort and plant the seeds.

Life is full of individuals who are always going to do something. They say they will do something, accomplish something, or finish something "one of these days." They are the kind of people who say, "I'm getting ready. I'm preparing, and one of these days I will do what I want and have what I need." They are always getting ready to do something, but actually never really do anything.

How about last New Year's Eve? Weren't you filled with resolutions? Well, chances are, those resolutions were soon forgotten. Why?

To truly have what you want and to become what you want to become, you must have a real goal. Goal setting is a very powerful process. The word goal is full of power. It represents gaining or achieving. Goals are earned in football, hockey, and soccer by teamwork, focus, and persistence. The goal in sports is a tangible thing like a net or goal post. In life, the goals are less tangible, but still require the focus and persistence. For the individual, one way to look at achieving is with a Guide to Overcome Attitude Limitations.

Teachers, more so than other professions, are more attuned to a goal-setting structure. Most lesson plans have goal components like objectives, outcomes, and rating forms for evaluation. The fact that you have a teaching certificate means that you went through a goal-setting process. When you decided to become a teacher, you examined the process that was necessary. You broke your plan down into segments of accomplishment: what to take each semester to obtain a bachelor's degree, when to schedule your practicum to student teach, and finally to complete the requirements for your state's licensure or certification.

Just as you accomplished your goal to become a teacher, you can apply that same approach to achieving desired results in other areas of your life. My suggestion is to set goals in terms of a total-person, holistic approach. First, look at all of the different components of your life. We have many distinct and interconnected areas such as: physical, mental, intellectual, vocational, and spiritual, as well as our financial concerns.

Goal setting can be a powerful and dynamic force in your life. Goals help you to determine a purpose, gain perspective, and stay focused on what really matters the most to you. Goals can give you a sense of direction and assist you in gaining more beneficial results from your endeavors. They can help you to take the steps necessary to turn your dreams into reality. To really make goal setting work for you, it is important to pay attention to the major areas of your life. This, too, then becomes a sort of juggling routine, just like you do while teaching. The diverse and many aspects of your life can be better managed if you know what you want and where you are going. That is the magic behind having a plan of action and then making the necessary changes you want to make in your life.

There are three essential questions to consider as you examine all of the major areas in your life: Where are you now? Where do you want to go? How are you going to get there? Take stock of where you are presently. Then determine where and at what level you want to be, and your plan of action then becomes the way you are going to get there. These three preliminary steps are much like planning your annual family vacation, which are planned in much the same way. The destinations you have reached in your travels were achieved in much the same way.

Goals that are written are more effective. By writing down your plans and aspirations, you are beginning a dynamic process that gains momentum as you more clearly specify what you want out of life. When goals are written down in a clear, specific fashion, they become more reachable because a commitment is made.

A written plan of action will become your guideline, your road map, to help you reach your destination. Be as specific as possible as you develop your plan of action. Gather the necessary information and resources to assist you, and set a timetable for the target date of completion. The time frame should include both short-term and long-term goals. This way, there is more of an incremental approach to breaking your goals down into smaller, more manageable parts. Set a realistic and flexible target date for achieving each goal.

Periodically, review your progress. Short-term goals can give you more immediate feedback and a better indication of how you are doing. This assessment phase can give you a sense of when and how you can accomplish your plan. For long-term goals, the review process can occur every few weeks or months.

It is advisable to be somewhat flexible in the goal-setting process. Although it is important to have clearly defined and specific goals, you need to remain open for any modifications or adjustments that may be necessary. Perhaps your time frame may be too ambitious or unrealistic. Make the necessary adaptations and press on.

Don't forget to reward yourself and take time to pat yourself on the back when you start to achieve your goals. This can increase your motivation and help you to sustain the effort necessary to obtain the results you want. Take pleasure in your accomplishments as a means of recognizing the time, effort, and energy you expended on the pursuit of your goals.

BRAINSTORMING

I have been a long-time advocate of the power and importance of brainstorming. I realize this valuable technique has been often overly emphasized and overused. I'm sure that many of you are tired of being in sessions in which trainers lead you through endless brainstorming sessions. It can even be viewed as trite, simplistic, and a hackneyed excuse for gab sessions or discussions. On the other hand, if done properly, brainstorming can be an effective method of developing greater creativity, cultivating ingenuity, and sparking innovation. Additionally, I have found brainstorming to be an excellent way to solve problems and make decisions. Good brainstorming explores different ways to look at problems so that we can open our mind to unforeseen possibilities. I value brainstorming as a way to generate more options, discover surprising alternatives, and increase the choices in our daily life.

In recent times, I have gained an even greater respect for what I call Individual Brainstorming. Now, I fully realize that the power behind using effective brainstorming is to generate ideas through others. The collective effort of a group of people can be far more successful than working in isolation. Still, many persons automatically dismiss its use if they have no one else available to generate ideas with.

I often do self-directed brainstorming. It is my way of opening my mind to see beyond the obvious, which is when I always seem to find alternative solutions. With my self-directed brainstorming, I have developed a keener sense of self-awareness and self-appreciation for the value of thought.

As you well know, the left and right hemispheres of our brains have long been thought to function differently and illustrate different preferences. Although, modern healthcare technologies, like CAT scans and MRIs, have shown that the hemispheres are not really that distinct, there are still left brain/right brain tendencies. How does this relate to brainstorming? Well, if there is no one else available to work with, then why not brainstorm with yourself within your own brain? Our left-brain tendency is to be analytical and sequential, to think in terms of words and to be logical. The right brain has a tendency to be more creative and visually oriented. The right brain also is more emotional. Why not let our left brain and right brain do their own individual brainstorming and then combine the two to better determine what to do or how to handle a situation?

TIME MANAGEMENT TECHNIQUES

I think that teaching, more so than other professions, requires extremely efficient use of time. In order to be as productive as you can be, learning how to better use time is an essential consideration. There are methods, techniques, and strategies that can help you to accomplish more in less time. Over the years, I have found a variety of helpful tips that have enabled me to be a better-organized and more efficient educator. I urge you, too, to make an effort to take these tips and adapt them to your own educational setting.

It is essential that you always have one planning calendar. The use of just *one calendar* can increase your efficiency. If you try to maintain more than one calendar, you have a greater chance of losing one or leaving an important appointment blank in one and not the other. In addition, you duplicate your efforts by writing the same information more than once. One central single calendar can do the job and be your source of organization and reflection. By using a planning calendar, you will have a point of reference, a focus, and a device to help you forecast future important events and get ready for your essential engagements. During any downtime that you have, you may want to glance through your planning calendar to reflect on upcoming events or projects that may be due in the near future. To be more effective, it is advisable that your calendar goes with you wherever you go, school, home, travel, even to the grocery store.

Time management experts have always recognized the importance of maintaining a planning calendar. With all our multiple responsibilities, a calendar is certainly a necessity. Yet I think that a strict adherence to a calendar can backfire at times. As a sign of being efficient, many of us quest for a calendar that is full and booked at all times. As we live our lives, it is common for the blanks on the calendar to get filled in quickly. This is especially true for teachers, who usually have all of the spaces filled.

As a start, I urge you to leave some blanks on your calendar. The more that we can get into the habit of deliberately leaving some open spaces on our calendar, allowing for more unplanned activities, the more we can get a sense of balance and a peace of mind. We will be able to keep our head above water and maintain a better perspective on our harried, fast-paced lifestyles. Use the blank spaces to catch your breath, to catch-up on your hobbies, or just do nothing at all. It will contribute to a feeling of peace and a calmness to realize that you have enough time to accomplish everything you want and still have time for yourself. Don't believe that it would be easy to wait until everything is done in order to allow more time for yourself. The reality is that you will rarely, if ever, find the time for yourself. The only way to find that time that you need is to plan for it. So, make an appointment with yourself and keep it.

Now, please don't get me wrong. This is not a way to shirk your responsibilities or to ignore important obligations. You need to recognize that you can only do so much in any given day and that if you try to do too much, it will be counterproductive. You will be inefficient, ineffective, and too tired to be of any use. This approach of taking time for yourself is actually a way of being more productive because you will be taking better care of yourself. Consequently, you can then be more effective as you tackle those obligations and complete those necessary assignments.

So take the plunge. Go to your calendar or day planner right now and, at this moment, decide to take better care of yourself. Look at your calendar and determine when to make that appointment. Note the dates and times that are already booked solid, and carefully decide when you can take at least an hour for yourself. That short hour will go very quickly, but since this is probably a new idea for you, you will want to start with smaller blocks of time. Find a date where you can free up that extra hour and devote it exclusively to yourself. Actually write your own name down and stick with it. Even if you get a call or a request from someone else to do something at the time you selected, you will now be more inclined to say, "I'm sorry. I'm already booked."

It's that easy. You will be amazed how productive you will be after you've come back from that time away from everything. You will also be able to expand the time frames beyond that initial hour. Soon you can be setting aside 90 minutes, two hours, half of a day. Not only will you feel more comfortable with the process, but it will also become an integral part of your routine. The magic behind this approach is that it will enable you to say to others who request your time, "I already have plans!"

If you feel uncomfortable with this approach, it's OK, because it's probably just something new to you. Once you get more accustomed to it and realize how it benefits you and others as well, you become an advocate of taking time for yourself. Remember, it is not selfish nor is it a way to hide from your responsibilities. It is designed as a means of increasing your efficiency by putting your life in harmony and creating the flow of hectic time versus down time.

Convince yourself that you are worth it.

In my opinion, time management is more of a system of developing organizational skills more than anything else. The more organized you become, the better you can use your time. By instituting a series of time-savers in your daily endeavors, you can better fulfill your teaching requirements and then have more time for yourself for fun and relaxation or for doing the things that you find enjoyable. Many teachers agree that one of their biggest problems is lack of time. You can get more done in less time by finding a better way to deal with all of your daily time constraints.

An important discovery for most new teachers is that they are never done with something. Teaching is an ongoing, never-ending process. You are involved in a profession that seldom, if ever, has a definite sense of closure or finalization. The continuous cycle of teaching is always moving, always evolving. The only semblance of any closure is perhaps the last day of school during a particular school year, yet, even that last day is not the end of the process. Teachers cannot say things like, "I'm finished teaching that student, now I can go on and teach the next one." You know that's not how it works. You are never done with teaching.

Once you realize the premise of never-ending teaching, you can gain a better sense of perspective and develop some time-saving tips to help you accomplish more.

1. Set priorities. The sooner you realize that you can't do everything, the better off you will be. Realizing that you are never done with your teaching duties helps you to gain a better sense of what's important right now to set daily and weekly priorities. Decide which activities, projects, assignments are really important to you right now and put the rest on hold. And learn to say "No" when you can.
2. Handle your mail, correspondence, and paperwork daily and only once. It is very easy to put aside those envelopes. Decide what needs to be done with the paperwork and make it a habit to take

the appropriate action that is necessary. The secret of getting things done is to do it now. Make it a habit to process that mail and correspondence at once. Merely putting it aside or leaving it in a stack accomplishes nothing; it's just putting it off and delaying necessary action.

3. Use waiting time for catch-up-time. Get caught up on your reading and planning; and remember to always have that reading file handy so that your wait time can be productive.

4. Keep your desk or work area as neat as possible. I know that this may seem unrealistic to you, but the more you can eliminate the time you waste looking for something, the more you can add to your available time. Plus, a desk or workplace that is not neat, with piles and messy stacks, can be distracting. If you are working on an important paper or project and your eyes wonder to that messy stack, there is a tendency to be distracted and to start thinking about that paperwork instead of the task at hand. By knowing where things are, you will be more organized and won't have to spend extra time looking for them. Keep the files and supplies that you use most close by and ready to use.

5. Prepare in advance for your next day of teaching. Set things out beforehand. Develop a routine where your next day's attire is readily available and your briefcase always in the same spot. And what about those car keys? Keep them in the same spot everyday, so you don't waste time trying to find them. Check the weather report the night before you leave so you can be better prepared, for instance, with an umbrella if you will need it. Keep your school paperwork in the same place at home so it is easily accessible. By spending a few minutes in this fashion each evening, you will develop more peace of mind that you are ready to go. You should then sleep better too, with more peace of mind.

6. Take charge of those interruptions. Identify your time-wasters and eliminate them. Using an answering machine or voice mail at home can put you in charge of those phone calls. You will be able to schedule the return calls on your schedule and at your convenience.

7. Avoid procrastination. It's very easy to put things off and delay taking the necessary action. Monitor your procrastination habits and make an effort to improve doing it now rather than later.

8. Schedule some leisure time for yourself—relax and recharge. This is your reward. Teachers especially need some downtime, some private time to recharge and reinvigorate their psyches and to gain some momentum for their next challenge. So, know when to take it easy for a while and regain that necessary strength and energy to get back at it with renewed vim and vigor.

SOMETIMES YOU JUST HAVE TO MAKE THE TIME

Today, everyone's schedules and calendars seem to be booked. It is common practice for many families to post a calendar listing of all the obligations, commitments, activities, plans, and personal agendas of different family members. It seems like everyone is in a hurry to get somewhere, and, often, there just isn't enough time in a single day to accomplish what needs to be done.

If most people are affected by this rush for time and a growing sense of urgency to get somewhere or to do something, then, no doubt, it is even further compounded for someone like you—a teacher. There are practical ways to maximize your performance and productivity, and you will be able to maximize your talents and find those pockets of time to stretch your days. You will then be able to get more done in less time and streamline your efforts.

Sometimes it's necessary to just stop and catch your breath. Only then can you make a conscious decision to do nothing else at that moment except what is necessary or what you want to do. Perhaps you have heard of towns that literally shut down for one evening. The media covered these strange events extensively for a time. Everything was cancelled to allow for nothing but family time. Families spent time together, not in organized activities, but in relaxing fun activites: playing games, doing crafts, making food, and so on. The purpose was to step off the fast track to do nothing but relax.

Those nights off for many towns were the result of many citizens finally realizing that they were overextended and overscheduled—that they were really attempting to do too much. Only so many things can be done in one day. The reality of having such a night is that it has to be planned and scheduled. In other words, it had to be scheduled right into the calendars.

I am quite impressed with those efforts. On one hand, it's a shame that our society has become *that busy.* It's a grand gesture to show the importance of making the time to do nothing. What I liked the most about this initiative is the emphasis that was put on the planning to accomplish the collective effort to do nothing. In much the same way, you and I can plan a "do nothing" day. We don't need a resolution from our local government to accomplish the same thing.

We, too, can build into our schedules a special time to kick back and relax. Mark your calendars on a regular basis. If you want to do something or be able to find the time to accomplish what you want to accomplish, then you must plan accordingly. Remember the old saying "plan your work and work your plan?" I strongly suggest that you, too, build into your busy schedules some time for yourself and your family to literally do nothing but relax. Make the time and take the time to unwind, let go, loosen up, and to sit down and rest for a while. This will enable you to recharge yourself and to become reinvigorated. You will then be able to get up and go with new gusto and the resolve to make new things happen.

You and your family or significant others deserve it. Yes, it is possible to find the time to become more balanced and more in tune with your life. You've earned the right to slow down occasionally. You don't always need to be that super-person who takes on all challenges and all offers to do something. My main point is to do what is necessary to put some balance into your life. Granted, none of us have a magic wand where we can just waive away our responsibilities. We need to be ready to do what is necessary, but, at the same time, we need to listen to our inner voice. When you start to get those messages to slow down and regroup, listen carefully. When you come back to reality, you will be refreshed and even more committed to your plan of action. We are always thinking of something that needs to be done or something we wish we could have done, or regretting the things we've failed to do. If we can achieve that balance, our perspective will change, and we can make the connection of all of the tenses of life: past, present, and future. Learn from the past, live in the present and enjoy it, and plan for tomorrow, but remember to keep the three in their proper places. And, by all means, don't be so busy that your life passes you by. You can do it; make it happen, and make things happen!

THE PAPERWORK AVALANCHE

Teachers are certainly dealing with increasing amounts of paperwork. This avalanche of paper that comes your way can sometimes be overwhelming. If there is one thing that teachers have in common, it is paperwork. Just think of all the forms, files, documents, papers, tests, memos, letters, and correspondence that are heaped upon you every day. And with all of the impending educational reform movements that are pending, many of them have new forms, new record keeping and a greater deal of documentation than ever before.

It is very common to let the paperwork pile up, so easy to look at something and to put it aside. Over the years, I have developed a simple, yet effective system to respond to the paperwork that comes your way. Next time, try this approach in dealing with your paperwork—the 5-D Approach:

1. Determine
2. Decide
3. Do it NOW
4. Delegate
5. Dump It, Discard It, or Designate It to a File

I believe that the secret to getting things done is to "Do it NOW!" The more that you get into the habit of following the 5 Ds, the more it will streamline your approach to dealing with paperwork. Plus, it can cut down on the amount of time that you spend looking for something.

HOW TO COMPLETE A MAJOR PROJECT

There is nothing so fatal to character as half-finished tasks.

—David Lloyd George

Our greatest weariness comes from work not done.

—Eric Hoffer

As a busy educator, you often do not have the luxury of having large blocks of time at your disposal. In addition to your hectic teaching schedule, you also handle multiple responsibilities and fill numerous roles. I recommend that you take a close look at your life and begin to departmentalize the diverse areas of your interests and responsibilities. Although improving your professional life is the focal point of this book, the other areas of your life that you are juggling also make up who you are. Besides your career, you still have your family, social life, civic activities, union obligations, religious and spiritual needs, as well as your avocations—hobbies, recreation, and special interests. You only have so many hours in a day to accomplish what you want to do effectively.

Many of us go through life with a broken record message of "Someday I will, or someday I will be able to do this or do that." Time has a way of quickly slipping by, and if you find yourself procrastinating or waiting for better conditions before you do something, chances are you will be spinning your wheels and never have the time to get around to doing what needs to be done.

I often use myself as a prime example. For most of my adult life, I wanted to earn a doctorate degree. One of my ambitions was to have the distinction of completing a doctorate program primarily for a sense of satisfaction and accomplishment. As I look over the decades of my life, I remember saying for years and years, that someday I would earn the title of Doctor. For many years I would only talk about it and never took the action necessary to even begin my studies. I have to admit, it was easier to talk about it or dream about than to actually take the initiative to earn the degree.

As I found myself getting older and as each year went by, I became distraught because I had at one time told others that I would earn a doctorate degree by the time I was forty. Before I knew it, I was four years past my so-called goal. It was easy to say that my intentions were good; I had made some progress in the pursuit of my degree and I had distinguished myself professionally in other ways.

In my particular program of study, there were several sequences of classes that had to be completed prior to beginning work on the traditional dissertation. So, as I took class after class, semester after semester, I felt that I was truly making progress. Things looked good for the goal to become a reality. However, upon completion of the all the required classroom work, I found myself procrastinating for almost three years as I stalled on the all-important dissertation.

Even as I avoided the dissertation, I began to feel worse, and I made all kinds of excuses for not doing my research. I even had an aversion to driving in the vicinity of the university or avoided going to the part of town where the campus was located, lest I run into someone from there that I knew. As each year passed me by, I thought that maybe it wasn't too bad to be an ABD (All But Dissertation). Then I recalled that during my career, I must have met well over 100 educators who called themselves ABDs. As I dwelt on my "unfinished status," I knew that I didn't want that to pertain to me. In addition, I remember how I felt each April as I read about yet another commencement ceremony at my university.

At about that same time, I received a note from my research advisor. The head of my dissertation committee wrote this message: "Tom, I haven't seen you for a very long while. Are you making any progress on your dissertation?" Wow! That note had a great impact on me. For one thing, I realized that it had actually been almost three years since I last met with him. I think it actually inspired me to take some kind of positive action and get something done so I could save face with my advisor.

So I woke up one morning and realized that I was 44 years old, still regretting that I hadn't earned my degree in the time that I had hoped. Finally, I decided to quit making excuses and vowed anew to begin working on a new dissertation. My first effort was to start applying some of the same motivational principles and goal-setting techniques that I often teach in my professional development classes and seminars. Rather than just reading about yet another graduation ceremony in the newspaper, I cut out the article and the photographs, made copies, and then displayed them in prominent locations throughout my house. This goal poster helped inspire me to take some action and quit procrastinating. At about that same time, I went to a local card store and bought a greeting card that said, "Congratulations on earning your doctoral degree!" I took the card home, signed it, dated it, and wrote this caption: "To Tom, Get busy and work on that dissertation so you can graduate! From, Tom." I displayed the card in my office so that I would have to see it each and every day.

I also took the newspaper articles and photographs on the university's graduation ceremony one step further, as I pasted my own photograph onto the picture. These goal-setting strategies set the stage for me to force myself to complete the work I had been putting off. Rather than just "spinning my wheels" and always being one of those ABDs, I started the real work on my dissertation and was on my way.

I want to stress the importance of having received that handwritten note. When I opened the envelope and read his note, it both motivated and embarrassed me to a great degree. Just the fact that he wrote to inquire and to check on my progress meant an awful lot to me. When I returned to his office for my long overdue appointment with him, I thanked him for the note and told him how much it meant. I also made a mental note that I would remind him of that note on my graduation day.

I feel that I was fortunate enough to realize in time that my life was passing me by and that time was slipping away while I did nothing to earn my degree. I also was lucky in that I had sense enough to have a wake-up call in my mind, as I realized that I was merely making excuses and avoiding the work necessary to earn the degree. Now, I want you to know that if you have some goal or aspiration that you want to do, it can be done.

Here are some effective strategies to use when dealing with and, more importantly, completing a large, seemingly impossible project.

When I finally realized what was delaying my action and causing my procrastination was that I was looking too much at the big picture of the dissertation, I changed my perspective to view not the entire project, but each smaller section instead. So, use the all-important premise of "one page at a time" or "one chapter at a time." Break each project into reasonable, surmountable logical steps.

When I realized that I could finish the dissertation in small steps, one page at a time, I felt a sense of confidence and relief, as I finally knew what I needed to do to get done. Wow! What a relief! Suddenly I didn't need a whole block of time at one sitting to work on my writing. I could just break it down. It was that simple. Now don't get me wrong; a dissertation is not a simple project, yet the simplicity of working on it bit-by-bit is what enabled me to successfully finish it.

In addition to the page-by-page breakdown of the task, I also realized that day-by-day, it was necessary to stay busy and do something productive related to the project. So, another strategy that worked well for me was that I made a contract with myself. I actually wrote on a yellow legal pad, "I, Thomas F. Staszewski, will devote at least 45 minutes per day to my dissertation. I will work on my dissertation each day and I cannot go to sleep unless I put in at least 45 minutes daily." I signed it and dated it and displayed my contract so that I would see it every day.

This pact of staying awake until I invested at least 45 minutes worked wonders for me. I even made signs and posted them throughout my house. On each bathroom mirror, on the refrigerator, and prominently displayed on the top of each T.V. was this sign:

> Tom: 45 minutes on your dissertation before you go to sleep!

These reminders triggered me to take a proactive, motivated approach to accomplishing my goal. I'm convinced that by setting goals with a specific date, breaking it down, piece by piece, word by word, page by page, is how I, and you, can complete any task you set out to complete.

The sign on top of the T.V. sent me a clear message that I must do the most productive thing possible at any given moment in order to finish what I started. I also selected some inspiring quotes that I put on my bulletin board. These quotes reminded me that I needed to finish what I started and that I should not give up:

> With ordinary talent and extraordinary persistence, all things are possible.
>
> —Thomas F. Buxton

> There are no secrets to success. It is the result of preparation, hard work, and learning from failure.
>
> —Colin Powell

> How many a man has thrown up his hands at a time when a little more effort, a little more patience would have achieved success?
>
> —L. Ron Hubbard, author

> Perseverance can do anything which genius can do and very many things which genius cannot.
>
> —Henry Ward Beecher

Well, on graduation day, I was able to reflect on my accomplishments. On one hand, I knew that I had missed my original goal by four years, but as a 44-year-old doctor, I was very proud as I heard my name read aloud by the university president. During the hooding ceremony as my research advisor assisted me with my robe and academic regalia, I reminded him how much that handwritten note meant to me. I thanked him for sticking by me and told him how much I appreciated his time and effort.

Another important point for consideration is the impact that a caring teacher can make on a student. In this example, the teacher, my research advisor who took the time to send me the note, was dealing with an issue important to the student, this doctorial candidate. Yet, in my case, the note was a clear signal that he still cared and was concerned about my status. The influence that a teacher has can be quite profound. So, as teachers, take the time to prompt your students, to remind them about important, ongoing projects and goals, and to inquire about how they are doing. That extra time and effort you make can be of great benefit as you continue to make great strides with your students.

Quit putting off those important projects. Stop making excuses and decide to finish what you have started. You don't want to be one of those people who are always going to do something. Eliminate wishful thinking and choose to do what is important to you and do it now! Always remember the Power of TNT: Today Not Tomorrow. Life has no guarantee that the elusive tomorrow will even come. Take constructive action today, get busy, and make the decision to accomplish what it is you want to accomplish. Your only regret can be that life has passed you by and that you didn't fulfill those aspirations you had. You don't want to look back at your life and say, "If only I had. . . . " If something is important to you and is a goal you want to achieve, go for it! Develop a plan of action, set a target date, and persevere. Never give up until you reach it.

5

CREATIVITY

I am enough of an artist to draw freely upon my imagination. Imagination is more important than knowledge. Knowledge is limited. Imagination encircles the world.

—Albert Einstein

Teachers are amazingly creative. It's just that the popular image of teachers and the profession of teaching is more along the lines of hard facts, accepted practices, and proven methodologies. However, many overlook the necessity for creativity, ingenuity, resourcefulness, and innovation that teachers practice and display on a daily basis. It is called the Art of Teaching, after all. Often, teachers do not give themselves credit for the immense amounts of creativity that they possess. Your imagination is constantly on display as you organize your classroom, design your bulletin boards, plan lessons, utilize the limited materials you have available, and find new ways to help students learn. In this era of restricted budgets and limited resources, teachers often have to create their own teacher-made materials.

The evidence of creativity is everywhere. As I visit teachers on their own turf, I see halls decorated with school themes, bulletin boards getting changed regularly, and classrooms showing the individual talents and interests of the teacher who practically lives there. In addition, learning stations, discovery centers, and the overall appearance and innovation of the work areas are all evident reminders that teachers are a very creative lot.

Still, what is displayed is just a fraction of the potential that exists within all of us to be creative. I have been studying and experimenting with the creative process for a number of years. Years ago, before I took serious note of the creative process, I was limiting myself through my own self-talk. I was commonly saying to myself such comments as, "I am not creative," "I am not artistic," "My imagination is limited," "Other people are more creative than I am," or "Creativity is not in my genes." All of these negative affirmations restricted any potential that I might have had to be creative. Now I am convinced that creativity is something that all people can improve on, expand, and develop to even greater heights. The old saying, "You are limited only by your imagination," is undeniably true.

I often have opportunities to visit downtown urban areas of large cities. Each time I visit a new city, I am impressed by the unique features and characteristics that each city has. I am in awe of the buildings, skyscrapers, and the architectural flavor of the area. Similar to the way an architect comes up with an idea and creates it, we can do the same with our everyday situations. Each one of us is, in a sense, the architect of our own situations. We construct our thoughts and ideas using our imagination and make them, if you will, a dwelling from which we operate. Very often, however, we can dismiss the ideas we think of and dismiss the opportunity to work with the idea and see where it takes us. The next time an idea literally pops into your head, be careful, allow it to be considered, work with it for a while, and, of course, write it down so that you will better remember it. Those ideas that we get are there for a purpose. They are sparks of imagination that could take us places we never thought possible before, if we would only listen and allow the idea some time to develop.

How about this refreshing perspective? Instead of saying to the class you need to cover a particular concept, try using the term "DIS-cover." I think that it can make a difference. The more you can create suspense, intrigue, or mystery, sometimes just by altering your vocal tones or by speaking more enthusiastically, you can rouse the curiosity in your students. Remember, most young people today are already overstimulated. They have developed a highly sophisticated limited attention span, so they can selectively accept or reject input. Try ways of creating interest—"Class, let's discover this together. I want you to know why this is important." You just might have a more attentive audience.

Remember, creativity has no boundaries. Creativity has no rules. The more you can be open with your thoughts and go with the flow of creative thinking, the more you will amaze yourself. Creativity is a process that deals with experimenting, taking risks, inventing new things, bending the rules, making some mistakes, and, above all, having fun. Being creative is indeed fun. It is a good feeling to go beyond the obvious. Try some of these suggestions as you exercise your creativity:

- Be willing to see things differently.
- Generate multiple options and alternatives.
- See different things . . . beyond the obvious.
- Develop a higher level of awareness.
- Know your thought process and how you think.
- Be more open-minded and get a broad-minded perspective.
- The first rule of creativity is: There simply are NO rules!

WAYS TO ENHANCE YOUR OWN CREATIVITY

This section contains suggestions to help you tap into your creative side and more fully realize your own potential. Give these six steps a try to discover some new possibilities:

1. Do some mental gymnastics. Our brains, like our bodies, need ongoing and regular exercise to function better and to stay alert. Working on puzzles, brainteasers, and other mental challenges can benefit you immensely. Brain calisthenics can work wonders!

2. Read more each day. Granted, your time is limited and you often don't have the luxury of much spare time to catch up on your reading. If that is the case, then "chunk" your reading into more manageable parts, ten minutes here and fifteen minutes there. A regular reading program can be a form of mental exercise that

can stimulate and inspire you. You will also expand your knowledge base and give yourself new ideas. This can enable you to make better mental connections on the path to an increased use of your creative process and also jump-start your imagination.

3. Carry a small notepad and writing instrument around with you everywhere you go. You can then better capture that random thought or idea by recording it. Reread your notes later and expand on your ideas. Review those notes on a regular basis and act!

4. Make a state change—that is, do something different. Go for a walk, go outside for a few minutes, change your position in your chair, or move to a different location in your home or office. Don't always sit or stand in the same location in your classroom. Move around and circulate through your room. The change of environment can be good for you. Making some change from the ordinary routine can help shake up and alert your brain cells. Vary your routine to get out of your rut.

5. Listen to some classical music or some jazz selections. Music can enhance the creative process, as it taps into our emotional side. Plus, the rhythm of the music can actually affect our brain waves by stimulating them, helping us to think better and perform better. The emotional connection to music can be a powerful creative force with you.

6. Buy some toys or building blocks and simply play with them. Hand-held manipulates, like jigsaw puzzles, strengthen our spatial perception, whereas assembling various-sized parts, such as in a model, enhances hand-eye coordination as well. Remember how much joy these activities brought you as a child? Why not try it again and resort back to that carefree, relaxed state.

MOVIES, ENTERTAINMENT, AND FILMMAKING

Evidence of the use of imagination and creativity can be found in the world of entertainment—from major motion pictures and independent filmmaking to the advertisements you see every day. These multibillion dollar businesses are great examples of imagination in action.

Recently, I viewed a 2-hour biography special on Arts & Entertainment cable channel entitled, "George Lucas: Creating an Empire."[8] The documentary was described as the following: "From a small town in California, not very far away, a young comic book geek would rise up to become one of the most powerful filmmakers in the world." I watched in awe of his success and accomplishments. I was impressed by one of Lucas's statements: "You can't do it unless you imagine it; you can't do it unless you imagine yourself being successful at it." That statement made a tremendous impact on me. What a powerful perception of the magic of creativity and imagination. All too often, we set barriers on ourselves and limit the potential of our own ideas. Listen to your own ideas; don't dismiss them. Don't be so quick to feel they are meaningless and fleeting.

MUSIC

Music can be a powerful force. Simply by listening to music that we enjoy, we can adjust our current emotional feelings. I urge you to think about and explore how music affects you.

I first learned of the importance of music and its impact on our feelings by hearing about some "world class athletes" who listened to music as a way of getting ready for competition. These well-trained and conditioned athletes believed that they could gain a mental edge and a better performance level by listening to music prior to competition. As a part of their warm-up ritual, the athletes made sure that they had their stereo headphones on while dressing in the locker room and also during their stretching and warm-ups. The music influenced their mental fitness and inspired them to a better performance; in essence, it psyched them up to a higher level.

This use of music intrigued me and made me wonder how you and I could gain the same benefit in our everyday life. As I explored the topic and began to use music in my own life, I became a quick believer. Therefore, I encourage you to experiment with this approach. Find some music that you like and appreciate, and listen to it next time you need a boost.

I started to use music as a part of my preparation process for my speaking engagements. When driving to my presentations, I make it a point to listen to CDs that inspire me and make me feel more confident and ready to perform. Part of my routine is to listen to songs that help me visualize a successful performance. I have found that it works wonders. The music affects me in a positive way and helps me to be my best.

In addition, background music while working in my office is also helpful. Having the music on creates a better and more productive work environment for me. It's amazing how music can be a stimulus for better thinking, positive thinking, and an emotional balance with our mental and physical psyches.

Certain songs can be very inspiring and help you through difficult moments. One song that has a special significance to me is from the soundtrack of the movie, *Space Jam*, featuring Michael Jordan. I was first attracted to the soundtrack because of the connection to the legendary basketball star. "I Believe I Can Fly," sung by R. Kelly, is one of my all-time favorites. The words are so inspirational, and I often listen to the song when I need a burst of energy or a better frame of mind.

I have a fond memory of the day that an adult education student sang a very inspirational song during an assembly. Part of my career as an educator was devoted to teaching personal development courses at a community college, at which weekly student assemblies were held. At these meetings, each student who was enrolled in the program was asked to stand and give a progress report on his or her week's endeavors. The staff carefully selected one of the students to facilitate the meeting each week. At the beginning of the progress reports, the student selected as the facilitator, Robert, remarked how the program had given him new direction and motivated him to believe in himself. He then began to sing eloquently the inspiring verses of a popular song. Thundering applause followed and every person there seemed to be uplifted and energized.

Then Robert began to describe how my personal development class enabled him to gain self-confidence, belief in himself, and develop a positive attitude. I will always remember that day, as it acknowledged the good that we do as teachers. It was nice to be recognized by a student, and it's those special moments that make teaching so worthwhile. You know the feeling that occurs when someone says, "Thank you" or "You have made a difference in my life." That's what is so special about the teaching profession. Those kinds of compliments and acknowledgments are special and help us to keep going and do our best as teachers.

Music can have an impact on you. If you are having one of those bad days, make it a point to listen to some music that will influence you positively. If you have the luxury of a planning period or a short break during your teaching day, have some music on hand that you can listen to. While driving to work, listen to some music of your choice that will have a positive impact on you.

HUMOR—YOU HAVE TO LAUGH!

Sometimes, you just have to laugh. Humor in our lives and in our classrooms is essential. I am sure you have heard, "If you don't teach with humor, then the teacher becomes the humor." To avoid the risk of becoming the humor, you can use the tips and suggestions in this section to address the benefits of humor and discover why it is important to include a bit of humor in your teaching.

> Laughter is a form of internal jogging. It moves your internal organs around. It enhances respiration. It is an igniter of great expectations.

> —Norman Cousins

Humor definitely adds benefits to our daily lives. Research has determined that maintaining a humorous outlook actually helps us feel good. Laughter has many positive documented health benefits. Writer Norman Cousins, when hospitalized with a serious health condition, began watching comedies on T.V. His doctors could not believe the rapid improvement in his condition. He truly believed that laughter and humor assisted in his recovery. The resulting book, *Anatomy of an Illness*[9] describes his discovery. Cousins's book became a phenomenal bestseller and detailed his ability to overcome illness through laughter. This triumph of the human spirit stressed that the human mind is capable of promoting the body's capacity for conquering illness and healing itself. The author described his personal experiences to overcome a supposedly irreversible disease, as he took responsibility for his own well-being. After suffering adverse reactions to most of the drugs and treatments he was given, he decided to take matters into his own hands.

Through the power of positive emotions, he prescribed for himself laugh-provoking films and humorous books. His advocacy of humor led others to believe in the healing power of laughter.

Similarly, the 1998 movie *Patch Adams*[10] starring Robin Williams, fittingly depicted the importance of humor in the healthcare profession. Humor and laughter were responsible for improving the quality of life not only of the patients, but also of the staff and the medical students. Dr. Adams describes his struggles and triumphs in his book *Gesundheit: Health is a Laughing Matter.*

Hunter "Patch" Adams is certainly a unique medical doctor. Often described as a professional clown, his bedside manner is hilarious as well as compassionate. His approach to healing has brought laughter and hope to thousands. His works caught the attention of Universal Pictures, which produced the popular movie.

Initially the medical establishment ridiculed his approach. Traditional medical school personnel were opposed to his humor and humaneness. The curriculum insisted that doctors should always maintain a professional distance from their patients. Patch believed that the best therapy is being happy. Health is the result of living a happy, vibrant, exuberant life every single day. Healthful living comes about through wonder, curiosity, and love, and joy is more important than any drug.

In the movie, the dean of the medical school accuses Patch of practicing "excessive happiness." When he asked, "What are you doing?" Patch replies, "According to the *AMA Journal*, laughter increases endorphins."

Today, we know more about the benefits of endorphins and the significance of the mind in the healing process. There is now more of an acceptance of the power of humor and the value of laughter in improving our overall health and well-being. A humorous approach to life can lead to greater joy and contentment.

Now, how about in the classroom? The same kinds of benefits can be gained within your classroom. You can improve the quality of life for your students by adding humor to your lessons and by practicing excessive happiness whenever possible. Oh sure, you might say, "How can I be happy with the class I have?" And you've definitely have had enough of the "class clowns." You wish that they would be more serious about their studies, and you don't want to encourage any more of that behavior. But humor does have place in the classroom, and I have found that it is definitely advantageous to the learning process.

It's okay to take your job seriously. After all, teaching is a serious matter, and there are many stakeholders involved with the teaching profession—students, parents, administrators, politicians, and even the media. You certainly need to be accountable to the demands of the teaching profession. I will, however, offer some suggestions on how to take things a little less seriously and how to lighten up at appropriate times.

In this day of political correctness, it's a given that humor must and should always be appropriate and within the standards of professionalism. Still, you can find many opportunities to inject humor into a situation. So, if examples of humor fall within the standards of decency, political correctness, and appropriateness and do not ridicule or make fun of someone, then we should be pretty safe with using humor.

In addition to stress relief, humor at work provides many benefits. Appropriate humor has its place in the classroom, the faculty room, at staff meetings, and in most life situations in general. With your fellow faculty members, humor can solidify a group. Comedian Victor Borge once said, "Laughter is the shortest distance between two people." Laughing with your fellow teachers establishes more of a bond and helps in developing an effective working rapport.

Numerous studies verify the fact that humor can actually improve productivity. Humor as a part of the teaching profession can enhance the overall climate of the classroom and of the school. Humor can actually improve students' concentration and break up the monotony of most tasks. Humor can gain and hold the attention of others. It helps break down barriers, fosters the establishment of better rapports, and can help in conveying and retaining information. Laughter improves alertness and ability to focus.

In your classroom and in the faculty room, you can set the tone. You can also be instrumental in establishing an environment for humor to prosper. Humorous posters, Post-it Notes, memos, signs, and other items can lighten the atmosphere and diffuse tension. Bulletin boards displaying humorous items, such as cartoons, jokes, and funny quotations, can provide a source of entertainment and enjoyment.

If you feel that you may be lacking in the humor area, make a conscious decision to set the pace for a more humorous approach to your daily endeavors. Get started right away, start to lighten up your attitude, and quit taking yourself so seriously. If you agree that humor in your classroom or school is valuable, then begin to make some changes. Teachers do not need to be entertainers or stand-up comics. We just need to think of things in a more humorous fashion.

To start out, think of some funny or ironic aspect to a situation, event or item of topical interest. Share it with others to test your delivery or approach. Again, you're not entertaining on stage. You're just trying to begin using humor in a more routine fashion. Make humor happen.

We can choose to add more humor in our lives. I recommend that you continue to explore ways to amuse yourself to reap the benefits that humor offers. You can make a conscious effort to increase your humor quotient. Several sources of humor, such as comic strips, funny T.V. shows, laughing with friends and loved ones, going to comedy clubs, playing games, and just lightening up our attitudes, are good ways to further experience the wonders of humor. Make an effort to find humor in situations where you least expect it. Laugh at yourself more often and smile at more people.

In your role as a teacher, keeping a sense of humor is as important as preparing lesson plans or helping your students get ready for exams. A lighthearted approach in your classroom can work wonders. The use of humor is crucial to building successful relationships with students, parents, and colleagues. With humor, you can have fun in your classroom, and it helps you to tap into your creativity. It can add some joy into your life and help you through tough times. In the midst of a difficult situation, look for laughter. Tough times are a part of life and humor can be helpful in adapting to those difficulties. It has been proven that laughter and playfulness are powerful learning tools. Humor can be a way of preserving a positive perspective in the frequently harried and crazy world of teaching.

Remember when you were a child and how easy it was to laugh and find humor in our daily activities? Sure you do. As we get older, we tend to take ourselves too seriously. Go back to your childhood behavior and start to see the wonderment and amazement that life has to offer.

Recently, I became aware of an intriguing organization known as Laughing Clubs. One day while browsing with the T.V. remote, I saw a news broadcast entitled the *Laughing Club of India* on the local CBS network station. I was immediately captivated as the narrator described how groups of individuals get together on a regular basis to laugh. The Laughing Clubs are gaining in popularity all over the world.

"World Laughter Day" was created in 1998 by Dr. Madan Kataria, founder of the worldwide Laughter Yoga movement. The celebration of World Laughter Day is a positive manifestation for world peace and is intended to build up a global consciousness of brotherhood and friend-ship through laughter. Its popularity has grown exponentially with that of the Laughter Yoga movement and is celebrated in more than 50 countries around the world.[11]

> Humor is the great thing, the saving thing after all. The minute it crops up, all our hardnesses yield, all our irritations and resentments fit away, and a sunny spirit takes their place.
>
> —Mark Twain

Since teaching is such a stressful profession, laughter can be a magic elixir to lessen the stress. It might just be the right tonic you need to gain a new perspective on your daily struggles. I urge you to experiment on what makes you laugh. The more you are able to release endorphins, the body's natural painkillers, you will begin to feel happier and have a pos-itive outlook.

WHEN ALL ELSE FAILS, SOMETIMES YOU JUST HAVE TO LAUGH!

How many of the following stressful situations can you relate to?

1. You forgot to reset your alarm clock for daylight savings time.
2. After parking your car in the school lot, you accidentally dent a newly elected/selected school board member's car door.
3. You've lost the answer key to your final exam.
4. You just *now* found that urgent note from a parent, *three* days later.
5. Your picture for the school yearbook looks like you are sick and sleeping.

6. You accidentally drop a glass of orange juice all over the grade reports that are due for submission tomorrow.
7. The VCR destroys the 45-minute instructional videotape during
   its first two minutes and you have nothing else planned.
8. You receive a summons for jury duty in July (and you have a trip
   planned).
9. The new superintendent's only child is assigned to your class.
10. Over the weekend you had a dispute with an employee of a local
    department store. After school on Monday, during a parent con-
    ference, you now find out that employee is also the parent of one
    of your worst behaving students.
11. Your PC crashes and your PowerPoint presentation on your en-
    tire unit is erased. So much for technology in the classroom!
12. In a rush to get home from a long day at school, you discover that
    the driver you cut off from the lane of traffic is the school board
    president (who also recognizes you).

WAYS TO CREATE HUMOR IN THE CLASSROOM

A good laugh is sunshine in a house.

—William Makepeace Thackeray

Schools are natural settings for humor. Think about all the popular
sitcoms and movies that take place in school. Look for the absurdity
and parody of situations that occur in your classroom. Not only will
you feel better, so will your students. Your class will appreciate you
more if you can find humor in things that happen, and your reaction
to various circumstances will gain a newer approach to your daily endeavors.

The periodic use of humor can be a valuable addition to any learning
environment. Studies have shown that humor, when it is used appropriately, can be an effective strategy to enhance student involvement, to
offset apathy, to gain attention, and to assist in retention.

Humor in the classroom can contribute to a positive learning environment and produces a relaxing atmosphere. Humor can also help to reduce
tension and to offset potential volatile and confrontational situations. It can

be used as a means to diffuse a stressful incident and to place it in a better perspective.

Experienced teachers know how to use humor to motivate students to want to learn, to create cohesion, and defuse tense situations. Remember that humor is also a nonverbal process. You can use facial animation or a funny fact to make your point. By smiling, you can make lively expressions, and that lets you develop that sparkle in your eye.

At times, be willing to make fun of yourself. It's helpful to make yourself the target of humor, rather than to pick on someone else. Former President Ronald Reagan was an expert at the self-deprecating type of humor. Many of his speeches were sprinkled with jokes or with references that described himself in a humorous vein. Reagan had a knack for winning over an audience by making fun of himself.

Make it a point to remember that the use of humor can be an enjoyable addition to your classroom repertoire. The numerous benefits to yourself and your students are evident because of the enjoyment and pleasure that humor can bring. I'm not saying that your class needs to be like a comedy club, but at appropriate and opportune times, humor can enhance the climate of your room, and it can improve the morale and alertness of your students. Your students will appreciate your outlook and look more favorably upon you as a teacher. Plus, your days will go better, and you will be able to look back and reflect on the good that humor can do for you.

Over the years, I have made it a point to capitalize on the proper use of humor in the classroom. For instance, recently while I was conducting a graduate-level curriculum course, I turned my back to write something on the whiteboard and, unbeknown to me, the class played a trick on me. When I faced the class again, I was surprised to see that every student had placed on their nose a "red clown rubber nose." I quickly asked the ringleader, "where's mine" and then placed one on my nose, too. Then we all shared a laugh. This kind of humor break set a good tone for the rest of the class. We were all able to gain a group laugh and mutual chuckle and then move on to the course content. Lighten up and don't take yourself so seriously. Laughter does have value!

A day without laughter is a day wasted.

—Charlie Chaplin

6

CHANGE

No doubt about it, we live in an era of constant change and relentless uncertainty. How do you respond to change? How does change make you feel? What happens to you when you experience sudden and unexpected change? Never before, in the history of our public school systems, has there been so much change. Educational reform movements abound and reorganization is occurring everywhere and at all levels.

In your own classroom, you are probably more adept with the dynamics of your organization and consequently more comfortable with change as it occurs. In your typical day, things occur in your classroom suddenly, unexpectedly, and often dramatically. Your response to these conditions is important. Most often, if you just keep the momentum going, you can make it through your lesson, the period, or the designated time for the subject at hand. If you stopped your teaching or delayed your lesson each and every time something occurred, you'd never cover anything.

Our resistance to change is often based on the habits we have developed over a period of time. We all tend to get into a comfort-zone, a level of routine that we are accustomed to, merely because we've done it that way for such a long period of time. Each one of us deals with change in a different way. Granted, there are various stages that psychologists have identified that one goes through during a process of change. Yet, I am convinced that change is often related to habits and various customs that we are familiar with.

For instance, I have an example of change that recently happened to me. Upon arriving at my usual exercise facility, I was reminded that the usual location where towels were dispersed had closed and was relocated to a different area of the club. This change related to an established routine that I had followed for over 20 years.

Now, I realize that a matter like getting towels is quite insignificant, yet my point is that the sudden change led to the need for me to establish a new procedure and create a new habit. I referred to this matter as a sudden change, yet in reality it was announced and phased in over a period of time through the posting of signs and numerous announcements. Nevertheless, I didn't pay attention to the signs and ignored the announcements until the old towel center had actually closed. At that point, I suddenly realized that a change had occurred. I then had to locate the new towel center and develop a new routine to secure the towels upon entering the club.

Another recent example dealt with the difficulty I had getting online to check my e-mail. After about an hour of frustration, I placed a phone call to the ISP. I was then greeted by a message that said, "As we have been announcing for the past six weeks, TODAY is the day that we are upgrading our equipment." The reminder also referred to various U.S. Mail documents and periodic e-messages that had informed subscribers that the provider was going to be down on that day. That made an impact on me. Once I heard the reminder message, I then felt rather foolish that I had ignored all of their efforts to announce the change.

As you begin to be more aware of how you deal with change, you might find yourself contemplating the need to do something different or to make some adjustments in your own life. Change affects each one of us in different ways, yet, there are some similarities that many of us go through. For instance, there is usually some sort of contemplation that occurs; in fact, it's more like a period of precontemplation. You know the feeling, you find yourself thinking about changing. You really don't go beyond the thought, so that means you haven't done anything about it yet. There is a tendency to hang onto your current behaviors and a lot of rationalization occurs. It's kind of like wanting to visit a particular city but never going there. As you get more serious about changing, you may then begin to wonder if your efforts will really be for the better. A great deal of consternation occurs as you contemplate doing something differently or breaking away from your usual routine.

After those reoccurring contemplative thoughts finally get to you, you then begin to prepare for a possible change. At this point, you are ready and ambitious enough to make a plan of action. During this stage, it is a good idea to anticipate any stumbling blocks and plan accordingly. This preparation phase then sets the stage for you to develop a more specific plan.

As you know, after a period of planning, we need to take action. Therefore, this is when you work your plan and begin to take charge of your life! As you decide to change something about yourself or your lifestyle, you will acquire a new can-do type of attitude. After a while, your new set of behavior and resulting actions will become easier and easier. Before you realize it, you will then be maintaining the behavior that leads you to change. You will arrive at a point where your new behavior becomes internalized, and you will then be able to make significant changes in your life.

OVERCOMING ADVERSITY AND DIFFICULT TIMES

> I am still determined to be cheerful and happy, in whatever situation I may be; for I have also learned from experience that the greater part of our happiness or misery depends on our dispositions, and not upon our circumstances.
>
> —Martha Washington, First Lady

We all have our share of ups and downs. Life can be difficult at times. Each one of us goes through various periods of setbacks, defeats, downtimes, adversity, and hardships. When we are faced with challenges and difficulties, oftentimes it's a matter of not so much what has happened to us, but how we react to what happens to us.

Just like in our own personal lives, troubles can beset us in our roles as teachers. In our daily teaching activities, we experience a combination of success and failure. Being able to bounce back and regroup is a skill to possess. Oftentimes, as you close the door to your classroom after a busy and hectic day of teaching and leave your school building, you may feel defeated. You may think that the students are getting the best of you; you may begin to wonder if you are making a difference. Above all else, put that difficult day behind you and look forward to tomorrow.

As you return to begin a new day of teaching, approach it with the first-day attitude. View the beginning of each day as a new beginning, a new opportunity to make a difference. Adjust your attitude to anticipate a successful day of teaching. Expect that today will be a great day. This optimistic expectation is far better than beginning the day with a defeatist's attitude. Start fresh, start over, and renew your conviction to make today a better day than yesterday.

> Finish each day and be done with it. You have done what you could; some blunders and absurdities have crept in; forget them as soon as you can. Tomorrow is a new day; you shall begin it serenely and with too high a spirit to be encumbered with your old nonsense.
>
> —Ralph Waldo Emerson

In order to keep balance in your daily struggles, it is important to monitor how you react to difficult situations. How we react to important challenges that come our way can be a defining moment for us. The more we condition ourselves to react to great challenges with determination and conviction, we will be better able to face those difficult times. Keep your problems in perspective. Realize that they are a part of life. Everyone has his or her fair share of problems. As Rev. Bob Schuller says, "Tough times never last, but tough people do!"

One of my favorite sayings is "This too shall pass." I believe that is true of our problems. They come and go. When they arrive, they can set us back and cause us a lot of pain, anxiety, and worry. To show you the reality of this approach, think of a point in time, such as six months ago. Once you have pinpointed that "half a year ago" time frame, then ask yourself this question, "What was I worried about then? What problem was I faced with at that time?" Chances are you cannot identify what was bothering you then. Chances are you have long forgotten those problems. For the most part, the difficult times come and go.

This approach is not a lackadaisical, carefree attitude; it is merely a way to look at our life's challenges as a fact of life and to view them as opportunities in disguise.

> If I were asked what I consider the single most useful bit of advice for all humanity, it would be this: Expect trouble as an inevitable part of life, and when it comes, hold your head high. Look it squarely in the eye, and say, I will be bigger than you. You cannot defeat me.
>
> —Ann Landers

LIFE'S LESSONS

I highly recommend that you take time out, every so often, to reflect on what I call life's lessons, those momentous (or not so momentous) occasions in which we experience the discovery of something important, the sudden awareness of some fundamental truth, or a realization that suddenly hits and has a profound influence on your life. Think about a significant development in your own life, when something happened to you that you will always remember. You learned something important from a situation, and it has always been with you since.

I vividly remember a moment in my life that will never fade. While a sophomore, I played football in high school. Through my hard work and perseverance, I got a chance to be on the starting team. But, while being considered for the starting position, one day at practice, I severely injured my knee. That was it. The season was over, and I was scheduled for surgery. Naturally, I was feeling pretty sorry for myself and became quite angry about it. Well, soon after my return from the hospital, I found myself visiting my favorite aunt. The only problem was that she lived in a third-floor apartment. While struggling to climb the stairs and enduring much pain and discomfort, I ranted and raved about my predicament. "Why me? Why now?" I muttered. As I painfully maneuvered my way up the winding staircase, literally dragging my leg from step to step, I stopped to rest, and there it was. On the wall hung a sign that immediately changed my perspective and gave me a different attitude about my situation:

> I cried the blues because I had no shoes,
> Until I met the person who had no feet.

I certainly felt a little immature for my whining and complaining. I knew that I had learned a valuable lesson.

Later during my sophomore year in college, I was on the wrestling team. Once during an important tournament, I was declared the loser of a match. Following the allotted time periods, I remember the referee raising the hand of my opponent and declaring him the winner. I was in a state of confusion because I was certain that I had earned enough points to win. Well, the coach came to my rescue. My wise coach, Ed Onoroto, immediately protested the decision and asked for a review. After some deliberation and review, the referee declared that the score was actually tied and that there would be an overtime period.

Unfortunately, I was already in the locker room, disappointed that I had lost. I went straight off the floor in disgust. I completely missed the protest and review. Suddenly Coach Onoroto shouted around the corner and told me in no uncertain terms to "get back out there," keep wrestling, and win the match. Well, after the overtime period, I managed to score enough additional points to win. To this day, I clearly remember Coach Onoroto telling me, "Tom, remember this day and this situation because in life, you do not always get a second chance. In fact, most often, there are no second chances." To think I nearly blew an opportunity to win simply because I let my pride and anger get in the way. I won the match and finished the season. Perseverance is what got me out of that locker room. Listening to little life's lessons can make a big difference in the outcome of your career and life.

Earlier, as a member of that same wrestling team, I had learned another very important life lesson. One day after practice, I approached the coach and asked for a meeting. I told him that I was thinking about quitting because there was just too much going on in my life at the time, and that I didn't have the time to practice. In other words, I was looking for an easy way out.

I remember Coach Onorato's reaction vividly. He calmly said, "Tom, you have a choice. You will find in your life that people can decide to finish what they started or to just walk away from unfinished business. You will find that those people who complete what they began have more going for them, and they get more done and become more successful in life, compared to those who quit. Which one do you want to be? It's your choice."

The coach went on to show me three photographs hanging in his office. Below each photo was an inscription, "Could of Ben," "Should of Ben," and "Would of Ben." He then asked which Ben I wanted to be: the one who could have been great, the one who should have done something, or the one who would have been successful but quit. That was a powerful lesson for me. He said there are too many people in life who never amount to anything because instead of doing something, they have regrets of what could have been, should have been, or would have been. I decided to not quit and to stick out the rest of the season and complete my commitment to the coach and to my team members. Since then, I have looked back at Coach Onorato's sage advice and have made it a point to finish what I start and to not make excuses or to walk away from my responsibilities.

If you find yourself saying, "If only I had done this" or "If only I had done that," then you are prime candidate for an intensive course in life's lessons. I highly recommend that you take some time right away to reflect on the positive aspects of your life so far. Think about the lessons that you have no doubt already learned, but haven't yet put into daily practice. Think about how you can start incorporating those lessons into your life right now and how they are going to assist you in achieving the goals you have set. More importantly, think about how you can take advantage of a Life Lesson situation in shaping the lives of your students and your peers.

One of my favorite activities that I include in my graduate education courses is a project entitled, "The Best Thing I Learned in School." I often asked groups of educators to reflect on what was the most important thing they learned as a student. This has proven to be a powerful exercise. It never ceases to amaze me that very little, if any, of the school stuff such as subject matter or content area is ever recalled as being the most important. While working with thousands of teachers, I never once heard anything about curriculum content. It has always been the advice of mentors and role models, the adages of the past, and the profound tidbits of sage guidance that has made a difference. Some of the more popular responses have been:

"Treat others as you would like to be treated."
"Do your best."
"Be honest."

"Be considerate."

"Always be fair."

"Never give up."

"A quitter never wins; a winner never quits."

"Maintain positive self-esteem."

"Work hard to earn things."

"To get respect, one needs to give respect."

"Appreciate strengths and understand weaknesses."

"Be responsible for your own learning."

"Be true to your word."

"Be considerate of others."

"Do what's right."

I always share with my classes the sage advice of one of my high school football coaches, Mr. Donald Zonno. He told us, "When you get knocked down, get back up." On the football field, it meant to quickly regain your footing, go to where the ball is and continue playing until the whistle blows. Yet, his real hidden meaning had nothing to do with the 100-yard field. It had more to do with the 100 yards of life. When I really listened to what he was saying, I knew very well that he was talking about life itself. When life becomes a burden, keep going. When life knocks you down, pick yourself up and move on. "Onward and upward" was his real message.

So over the years, I practiced his advice. I would not let life's setbacks slow me down. I kept going. I would not stay down. I would pick myself up, brush off the dust and grime, and persevere. I never gave up, although many times I felt like it. I kept struggling and kept my head up high. Hang in there! That's the most important thing I learned in school.

As I listened carefully to the reports from practicing teachers as to what the most important thing they learned was, I was amazed at how much detail was apparent in their descriptions. They had clear and vivid memories of the advice that was bestowed upon them by one (or many) of their former teachers.

The name of the teacher, the event, the circumstance, the time, and place was precise in every aspect. These minute details were evident in their vivid descriptions and accurate recall. What a difference from math, or science formulae, or the spelling of words. No, I am not knocking these facts or minimizing the importance of the subject matter or knowledge

base associated with school. I just want you to recognize the profound influence that you, as an educator, can have on the mind of a student. Be
aware of how a bit of advice can carry over into adult life and continue to
influence that student years later. The powerful effect that a teacher has
is truly remarkable and utterly unquestionable. So remember, the next
time a student asks for advice or guidance, stick with your principles and
convey to your students the importance of what you know life is all about,
beyond the textbook and into the real world of the rest of their lives.

"It's important to be in shape and to be physically fit." I can still hear
those words today, some forty years ago. My life-long interest and dedication to physical fitness can be directly attributed to my father's sage
advice. Learning the fundamentals of exercise, calisthenics, weight
training, mental discipline, and the virtues of making a commitment to
my father has had a lasting impression on me. I am thankful that he
equipped a home gym for me to use while I was growing up. In addition, he showed me the ropes at the downtown YMCA. To this day, I
make it a point to stay in shape and exercise daily.

In addition to my interest in physical fitness, my zest for learning can
also be attributed to my mother and father. My parents always stressed
the importance of a good education. They always emphasized that what
you have learned and what you know could never be taken away. My parents convinced me that a good basic education and earning an advanced
degree would open many doors of opportunity—and how right they were.

As we reflect upon our lives, it is always a good idea to pause and remember those who have influenced us and helped us along the way.
These life's lessons have shaped and molded us. They made us into what
we are today. The fact that people cared enough to take the time to listen and offer advice or a tidbit of knowledge that made a difference
should always be remembered. Whether they are your parents, other
family members, friends, teachers, or merely acquaintances, we should
always remember them and be thankful for what they did for us.

In many instances, it was our teachers who have made the biggest contributions to our lives. Teachers have the unique opportunities to be at
the right place at the right time, when we were susceptible to learning a
profound truth or developing a new way of doing something. Perhaps
they sparked our interest in sports or an academic subject. Maybe they
boosted our self-esteem at a crucial moment when we really needed it. I

have offered only a few examples out of my own life. But I am certain that when you reflect back on your own experiences, you will be able to recall many instances where a teacher affected you in positive ways.

Recently, I had an opportunity to get reacquainted with a former teacher. One day while exercising at a local health club, I noticed one of my former coaches who had also been my health teacher. After reacquainting ourselves, I thanked him for all that he did for me. I stressed that what I learned from him was much more than just ideas from books, I told him that I learned a lot about life and how to be a productive citizen. I sensed that this display of gratitude and appreciation was happily received, and I'm convinced that both of us left that conversation with a good feeling and a sense of fulfillment.

As I look more closely at these life's lessons, I certainly want to recognize what my wife of many years, Linda, has done for me. I have a tremendous amount of gratitude because of all that she has shown me. I know how much I have improved just by knowing her. Early on in our marriage, I did not have as much empathy and understanding for others as I now possess. It was Linda who convinced me that every person we come into contact with is special and unique. She taught me that I should always be at my best while dealing with others. Linda also convinced me that we should always be appreciative of others and help them whenever possible. These lessons are important to me and have made a difference in my life.

MEMORABLE EVENTS

Each one of us, in our lives, has had special occasions, unique occurrences, and auspicious events that are truly memorable. They always stick with us no matter what else happens in our lives. Even with Alzheimer's patients, the mind still latches on to these memorable events.

I will always remember the day in 1978 when I met Arnold Schwarzenegger. At that time, he was known only to the weightlifting and bodybuilding culture. During that phase of my life, I was heavily into bodybuilding. I closely followed Arnold's career as he won numerous Mr. Olympia championships. Once, when he was near the area, I attended one of his book signings. I listened very carefully to him as he openly talked about his dreams, his hopes, and his aspirations.

Then someone in the audience asked him what he planned on doing after his bodybuilding career was over. To this day, I still remember his confident manner when he said that he was going to become the most successful actor and the biggest hit in Hollywood (and he wasn't referring to his physique). Some people in the audience chuckled and one said, "Arnold, what, you a movie star? Come on, you can hardly speak English." Again, he offered in a confident manner, "Just you wait and see!" In addition, he talked about earning a college degree, marrying a beautiful and famous woman, and maybe entering public office.

Today, we already know about his rise in the movie business, his high-profile marriage, and his political career. Well, enough said. Arnold was certainly right. He did everything he said he would, and then some. Talk about vision, determination, goal setting, and making things happen. Just as in his bodybuilding days, Arnold certainly does things in big ways. And he still carries himself with the same steadfast determination that he portrayed at that book signing.

To this day, Arnold continues to motivate and inspire others. He remains a strong advocate of education reform in California.

STRESS RELIEF

You can use many techniques and activities to relieve the constant stress in your life and in your job. Take a stress-less break and concentrate on any of the following anxiety relievers:

- Make time for play—real play.
- Daydream.
- Listen to the birds.
- Sing a song then sing it again.
- Play your favorite music.
- Stand up and stretch—limber and loosen up.
- Pause and look out the window. Look into the distance to stretch your eyesight.
- Go for a walk.
- Walk the stairwells instead taking the elevator.
- Count your blessings and be grateful for what you have.
- Call on an old friend or make a new friend.
- Change your coffee break to an exercise break.
- Go fishing—even if you don't fish!

- Build a model airplane or car.
- Massage your temples.
- Laugh out loud.
- Create a peaceful scene in your mind.

- Go to a baseball game or play baseball.
- Plant some flowers.
- Pet your dog or cat and take it for a walk.

With all the stress you encounter on a daily basis, you are placed in a situation in which at any given time, something can happen. The unexpected, unpredictable, and uncontrollable nature of the teaching profession can place a heavy burden on you. It will certainly be in your best interest to have more flexibility and adaptability in your outlook.

Stress has a way of creeping up on us, a little at a time, and on a daily basis, it all starts to add up. Through our frustrations, troubles, and difficulties, stress can continue to build within our systems. For the most part, stress is a neutral factor. Stress starts to mount because of the way we think about a situation or a circumstance that we identify as stressful. Thus, a major consideration is not so much the event itself, but how we react to the situation.

Although stress is mostly neutral, it can actually assist us in adapting to certain situations. Initially, stress can aid us in becoming more motivated, more alert, and able to more readily respond to a given event. It can sharpen our senses and add some zest to our life. In other words, initially, stress can give us a wake-up call and startle us to positive action. However, as we monitor our bodily reactions, all too often, the stress tends to mount within ourselves. Realizing that stress is unavoidable will help us to better cope with the difficulties that may arise. It can add to our perspective that stress is a part of life. Learning to cope with it can help to safeguard your overall health and increase your ability to enjoy life.

When faced with a buildup of negative stressful feelings, I have found that making various adaptations and adjustments in a more positive fashion means that I will be better able to diffuse anxious, tense feelings. The following are some tips to better manage stress in your life:

- Break out of your normal routine, do something different, and establish a change of pace.
- Don't let the little things bother you, dismiss them as minor inconveniences.
- Focus on the THIO affirmation: Today Has Its Opportunities, if you only look for them.

- Replace your negative self-talk with positive self-talk.
- Treat your self better; view yourself in a more respectful manner.
- Share your concerns with a trusted friend or confidante.
- Enjoy the simple pleasures of life; learn to better appreciate your surroundings.
- Focus on what's good in your life, on what you have, and not on what you don't have.
- Reserve some time for yourself, relax, and take it easy.

You also might want to take a look at your classroom and your teaching practices to see if you may inadvertently be adding to your stress. As you assess your classroom, ask yourself these questions:

- Is your room arrangement neat, efficient, and is it easy to maneuver through?
- Do you follow a normal routine so that your students know what to expect?
- Have you planned your teaching day to alternate between quiet time and active time?
- Do you have a good balance of activities, organized projects, and independent work, and offer variety in your teaching?
- Are you consistent in dealing with your students?

Getting a better handle on your classroom practices can give you more sense of control over your body's reaction to stress. It will allow you to establish a flow and a rhythm to your day.

The educational arena today is very demanding and requires much stamina. The classroom setting often has an uncertain atmosphere. Being ready for the unexpected and being able to maintain your composure under stressful conditions can be quite a challenge, but if you practice these techniques and exercises, you will be better equipped to cope with the unforeseen surprises that come your way.

STRESS IN THE CLASSROOM

Classroom management can be a cumbersome process at times. Depending on what your pupil/teacher ratio is, the likelihood of always maintaining the ideal calm, predictable atmosphere is pretty limited.

Human behavior is often unpredictable, and people (regardless of their age) do things that never cease to amaze me. Things happen to us that we have absolutely no control over. Despite this powerless condition, I'm convinced that we do have control over how we choose to react to a situation. Many stress management programs suggest that the more we monitor our reactions to outward occurrences and the more we are aware of our feelings, attitudes, and emotions, the better off we will be in reacting to stressful situations.

I recommend that you become cognizant of this choice factor. Then begin to take full ownership of your reactions. Remember, the choice is yours. You can choose to react positively or negatively and then experience the positive or negative consequences of your reaction. It is also important that you plan for rest and recovery from all of the demands you are faced with. The more that you can pace yourself and realize that at times you must slow down, kick back, and relax is an important factor in controlling your reaction to stress and the unexpected. It's essential to settle down between stressful situations or events. This downtime is beneficial to recharge yourself and to regain your momentum for the next stressful circumstance.

So, get into a habit of taking mental breaks to unwind and relax your mind. If something out of your control threatens to upset your balance, forget about it. Everything's going to be all right. Give yourself a pep talk, and maintain that positive attitude to regain your stamina and boost your energy level. These periods of rest can be moments when you let your mind go and sit back for a while. Listen to your body. When you are experiencing stressful feelings, your body knows that it's time to unwind. Just as you plan your teaching times, exercise time, and family time, you need to schedule time for yourself to allow your body to adjust and adapt to the high pressures of teaching. Force yourself to take a break, even if it's for just five or ten minutes. Clear your mind, and take a break from the constant thinking about things out of your control.

TAKE A DEEP BREATH

Deep-breathing exercises can also be a beneficial means to relieving stress in your life. Diaphragmatic breathing is healthful and can be a calming factor in your daily endeavors. Too many people mistakenly think that deep breathing is only for yoga gurus, mystics, or spiritual teachers. It is actually something that anyone can do and can be extremely helpful in adding a balanced perspective. Next time you are feeling stressed or frustrated, try this approach:

1. Lie down or sit in an upright position and get comfortable.
2. Place your hands on your lower abdominal area.
3. Exhale.
4. Then, breathe deeply, focus on drawing your breath from your nasal areas through your lung capacity and down through your diaphragm (lower abdomen area).
5. As you continue this cycle, you will be better able to determine if you have been breathing from your chest area or from your diaphragm.

If you already are familiar with deep breathing through your diaphragm, then you know of its importance. Continue to practice this kind of deep breathing. Avoid shallow breathing through only your chest area. Increase the amount of air you inhale and exhale more deeply. This will help you to achieve a more calm feeling and aid in relaxation. As you continue to practice deep rhythmic breathing, you will become more aware of your faculties and more effortlessly achieve a better way to breathe. When your mind and body are calm, you are better able to think more clearly, increase your awareness, and tap into more of your wisdom through this approach.

HOW TO STAY CALM UNDER PRESSURE

Maintaining a calm demeanor when under stress and pressure is a skill in itself. Have you ever noticed how some people have a knack to remain cool and in control under adverse situations? These kinds of people have mastered the art of staying in charge and being able to react in a sensible way, even when the pressure mounts. To establish a better reaction to tough times and to respond with your best, even though you may be feeling your worst, it is important to do the following:

1. Take a deep breath; in fact, take several repeated, very deep breaths. This first step to better facing difficult times will keep you

in better control of yourself and the situation. In addition to allowing you some lead time to think through your reaction, deep breathing can also clear your mind and help to relax the major muscle groups in your body. You can respond better with a fresher mind and a less tense body.

2. Choose to remain calm and composed. Right, easier said than done. Well, the more you concentrate and commit yourself to staying more cool and composed, the more you will be. Remember the "act as if" premise. The more you act like something, a quality, trait, or characteristic, the more you will become it. In other words, act as if you are calm and you will become the result of your actions. When you are cool and calm, you will be better able to rise to the occasion and meet that difficulty head-on.

3. Think it through, even for a few seconds. Get a hold of your thought process and sort out your self-talk to be better able to respond in a productive fashion. We tend to react or overreact to difficult situations, rather than act the way we want to or should respond. If you continue to react only to stress, then you are allowing stress to control you. You have the ability and the choice to respond however you want in any given situation.

4. Establish a foundation of strength through a learned behavioral response. You can build a better sense of control by focusing your mind and thoughts and drawing inspiration from past successful events in your life. During those moments of anxiety and frustration, call upon your self-confidence to help you make it through. This, in a sense, is a performance cue, something that can trigger your mind to extract those past feelings and confidence, resurrect them, and apply that same level of emotion to the present moment.

5. Take action. You can focus yourself and deliberately channel your fear and anxiety into a more calm, positive, and deliberate action.

In many respects, these methods are similar to ones that skilled athletes use when they need to perform under pressure and to succeed. This psychological battle that occurs not only on the athletic field but in the classroom, too, can lead you to perform better when necessary. Just like a skilled athlete during competition, you, too, are in a sense of competition every time you teach a lesson.

SELF REHAB

Often in our lives, we find that even after we have tried everything, we still somehow come up short. One thing happens that puts you over the edge, beyond your level of tolerance. You have used every coping mechanism at your disposal and it's still not enough. Everyone has obstacles in his or her life that will seem insurmountable. And in some cases, they really are.

So, I have one more piece of advice for you. If you need help, go get it. If you find that something in your life is holding you back and making it more and more difficult for you to be productive and accomplish what it is you want to accomplish, look for ways to get assistance in what you are dealing with. If you are in need of changing a behavior or find yourself losing control on matters where you should be in control, then perhaps some sort of professional help may be what you need. If you need support, find a source, and then go get it.

I have always looked at life as a do-it-yourself project. I believe that we get out of life exactly what we put in it, and I am an advocate of personal responsibility and self-rehabilitation. This self-change approach to dealing with undesirable habits can work wonders if you are fully equipped to identify the problem, map out a plan, and implement the changes, but I also realize that you may not be as self-directed as I am and that the self-rehab approach may not be for you.

I respect and admire the trained professionals who are qualified to deal with matters of counseling, therapy, crisis intervention, and behavior modification. These professionals do offer important and vital services to those in need. And remember, do try to use the strategies I outlined here for you, but if you have one bit of doubt, especially when life-altering or even life-threatening situations are concerned, seek help immediately.

JOURNAL WRITING—WHY YOU SHOULD HAVE YOUR OWN JOURNAL

"What's in it for me?" you ask! Why on earth should I maintain a journal? Well, there are numerous benefits and advantages to daily journal writing. Thoughts can be better recorded. Quick observations and un-expected revelations can be written down for later contemplation. You might even find yourself considering writing for publication. This sec-tion is devoted to convincing you of the merits of journaling.

I must admit, journal writing was a new experience for me, too. For several years, I had been aware of advice about why it is important to maintain a journal. At first, I was unconvinced. I thought that I didn't have the time or that I didn't need it. Well, once I started and contin-ued to maintain my own journal, I was impressed. I suddenly found an outlet for those thoughts that came to me unexpectedly. I finally had a place to write down important findings, things that I read, things that I heard others say, and things that happened that I thought were signifi-cant. Now I am convinced there is merit in journal-keeping for you as well.

Think about it; for years, teachers have been requiring their students to maintain journals. Yet, probably most educators have never thought of how beneficial the process could be for them. I suggest you turn the tables, so to speak, and begin to capture your thoughts, ideas, and in-sights in a journal format.

If this is a new process for you, then a good beginning point is to pick up something interesting to use for your journal. You could use an ordinary spiral notebook, a 3-ring binder, a pocket calendar or planner with room for notes, or an actual bound book with blank pages. I keep a notebook with a built-in planner section with each day broken up into one-hour sections. I have found that it is now essen-tial for me to keep it handy and readily available. I can immediately get my thoughts and perspectives onto paper. I first dismissed the im-portance of maintaining a journal, but I continued to hear again and again the benefits of the process. I was sold, and now I believe that journal writing is a vital ingredient for personal development and growth.

Maintaining a journal enables you to monitor your own internal processes. This approach can be helpful as you integrate psychological perspectives into your personal development, and it can help you get a better handle on your thoughts, feelings, and emotions. Through a process of rigorous self-examination, you can better see the changing cy-cles of your life. I have also found that it helps you to remember your dreams, aspirations, hopes, and random ideas that appear virtually out of nowhere. How often have you suddenly had a brilliant idea as you pondered the meaning of some situation, event, or circumstance? All too often, these fleeting thoughts soon disappear, and we are prone to dismiss their importance. By recording those moments in your daily journal, you can begin to understand better and gain insight from them. Using a journal can connect you to your higher self—the part that deals with critical thinking, creativity, wisdom, and a deeper awareness of yourself.

Teaching is often a chaotic process, full of uncertainty and ever-changing conditions that can leave you uneasy at times. It's easy to lose touch with ourselves and get swamped in the busyness of our lives. Many of us actually hide behind scattered activities because we don't get in touch with our real feelings, and we don't know what we want our lives to be. By using a journal, you can turn your perspective on life from a seemingly meaningless, random succession of events into more of a precise, more finely tuned examination of your progression into wisdom. It allows you to keep track of your life's lessons, learn from them, and, more importantly, put them into practice.

I first gave the notion of keeping a daily journal some serious consideration upon reading that many sports figures keep a journal. Many say that it helps them reflect on their experiences, difficulties, and their overall place in the game. Writing is therapeutic for any profession.

By creating daily journal entries, it enables busy teachers, like yourself, to pause, gather your thoughts, expand on your ideas, capture your emotions, and reflect on things that matter to you.

Give it a try, I highly recommend journal writing as another avenue for you to explore in your pursuit of being the best teacher that you can be. It will allow you to articulate your thoughts into a written format for a record of your own personal growth and development. What you discover may amaze you. You will be glad that you've invested the time, effort, and energy to maintain your own personal journal. The returns on your investment of time are many. This practice will benefit you as you continue to become the teacher that you want to be and were meant to be. You can do it. Get started tomorrow and you will be glad that you did.

REMEMBER THE IMPORTANCE OF PLAY

It is paradoxical that many educators and parents still differentiate between a time for learning and a time for play without seeing the vital connection between them.

—Leo Buscaglia, author, lecturer

The older we get, the more we tend to ignore our playful sides. For some reason, many adults feel as though they have outgrown their need to have a good time and to enjoy life. We recall fond memories of childhood and the countless hours we spent in play. Oh, how I still remember my favorite toys and the sheer pleasure I derived from just playing. In our younger days, we naturally set about amusing ourselves with various toys, gadgets, or common items we found. As adults, we tend to take ourselves too seriously and even avoid cracking a smile. How unfortunate that many of us have put those carefree, childlike days behind us.

As you look at ways to achieve a better balance in your life, remember those days. At that time, we were carefree and void of any worry. As a means of diffusing some of the stress currently in your life, give some consideration to taking some time to play. Now, I am not talking about shirking your duties and responsibilities or walking away from your important personal and professional obligations. What I am saying is that, from time to time, you may want to look at adding some playtime to your day. Too often, we can get so bogged down in our daily routine and all of the activities that fill our days. Why not take some time to explore your creative and imaginative side, as you engage in some playful type involvement?

There is a trend in this country to encourage busy adults to schedule some periodic playtime into their hectic schedules. In fact, many companies, businesses, and organizations now recognize the benefits of occasional play-breaks interspersed into a daily schedule. Many corporations encourage employees to take some playtime and use children's toys, like Playdoh and Etch-A-Sketch, as a means of relieving stress and as a way of fostering creativity and imagination.

This is a refreshing trend. It's quite important to loosen-up occasionally and effect a change of pace in our hectic daily regimes. I encourage you to look for ways to include some periodic playtime into your busy day. Make an effort to schedule some downtime for you and your family to experience this kind of joy. Perhaps an area in your house could be devoted to some space to have some toys on hand for you to use. Often, just a few minutes away from it all is enough of a diversion to refresh your mind and your spirit.

What about that faculty room at your school? Over the years, I've been in my share of faculty rooms and teachers' lounges, and, no doubt, some of these areas are in need of lighter fare. If the designated room in your building is in need of an attitude adjustment, why not bring in some toys or novelty items as a way of relieving some of the stress and strain of an adverse day. Give it a try! See what develops. Perhaps a yo-yo, modeling clay, some juggling balls, or a game of checkers—anything different may lead to a more relaxed atmosphere and foster some "teacher bonding."

I still remember to this day how enjoyable I found a couple of sets of ping-pong to be. At one middle school where I used to teach, several colleagues and I regularly played a few games of ping-pong to alleviate some of the tension of our hectic days. We made it a point to let off a little steam, as we engaged in a little bit of play and frivolity during our matches. The kinesthetic movement and the thrill of a bit of competition worked wonders for us all.

Just a few minutes a day devoted to some play or manipulating a toy may be all you need to go back to your classroom for that next class in a more refreshed frame of mind. Try it. It works!

WHAT DO YOU DO FOR FUN?

"Fun," you may say, "What's that? I'm too busy to have any fun." Well, I believe that one way to offset stress in these all too stressful times is to develop a more playful attitude, find a new zest for living, and, at times, act a little on the goofy side. Each one of us has our own definition of fun. I encourage you to reflect on this question: What do you do for fun?

If you have to stop to think about it and wonder when was the last time you had any fun in your life, then perhaps you need to add some fun to your outlook. In this section, we will explore ways to develop and maintain your own FUN FORMULA. This FUN FORMULA, if you will, is a way to intercept potential anxiety and change a stressful situation into a more manageable one. You need to have an even keel, a brighter outlook, and a carefree attitude to make it work. Don't get me wrong. I'm not saying that you should develop a cavalier attitude about serious situations or circumstances, nor am I not saying to fluff-off our problems and difficulties. What I am saying is that you and I can do things that we enjoy and enjoy them more fully, if we can develop a fun-type attitude and thus be better able to cope with the demands of the teaching profession.

Spelled out, the FUN FORMULA looks like this:

Forget about it!

Understand, unleash, unlock.

No! Learn how to say, "No" to those who affect you negatively or take without giving back.

Funny—keep thinking funny.

Outlook—keep your outlook fresh.

Reinforce your feelings with the affirmation that "This too shall pass."

Motivate—yourself and others.

Use your gifts and talents to make a positive impact on the lives of those around you.

Learn something new everyday.

Attitude—keep that positive attitude.

> Play is often talked about as if it were a relief from serious learning. But for children, play is serious learning. Play is really the work of childhood.
>
> —Fred Rogers, T.V.'s Mr. Rogers

REMEMBER TO SAY "THANK YOU"

My mother always told me that it is important to say, "Thanks." Today this vestige of old-fashioned politeness is often overlooked. Whenever a sales clerk thanks me for my business, I feel good. I tend to return to those businesses or establishments that recognize me and appreciate my being there.

A nearby car wash posted this large sign near its exit:

> *Thank you for being our customer.*
> *We appreciate your business.*

Whenever I drive away from that car wash, I am glad that I have a clean car, but I also feel good when I read the sign. In addition, the workers are friendly and engaging and often say, "Thanks for being here."

A sincere thank you is hard to find. It seems as though many cashiers do not even say a word today. In an informal personal survey, I found that many cashiers failed to say "thank you" after the sale. More often, my change or credit card slip has been handed to me in dead silence. Not a word of thanks, or a "Have a nice day." It's almost as if I have interrupted their day by paying for my purchase. I don't know about you, but I find this discouraging. My point is that if we are not even getting a "thanks" today for being a money-spending customer, then, as teachers, our work is becoming more and more thankless.

One of my inspirations for writing this book was to be able to thank you for being a teacher, sharing your expertise and your knowledge with your students. Thank you for showing all of your students a high level of acceptance and approval. Your words of wisdom, as well as the encouragement and the gestures of kindness that you extend to your students, need to be recognized. The positive influence that you have on your students is noteworthy and the fact that you answered your call to be a teacher should be proclaimed. Your students need you; your community needs professionals like you. Your contributions are immeasurable. You have made a difference. Your lessons are permanent. You are very important and the world is a better place because of you.

One of the most gratifying aspects of being a teacher is when a current or former student takes the time to say thank you. We remember vividly when our students who have thanked and acknowledged us for our efforts. On a larger scale, there are some fine examples of how gratitude has been extended to teachers. Tom Hanks thanked his teacher at the Academy Awards, and Rashaan Salaam, the Heismann Trophy Winner, thanked his teachers, as well.

7

TAKE CARE OF YOURSELF

After a hard day of teaching, and even though you still have lots of work to do to get ready for another day, take a few moments to take care of yourself. Plug one of following tips into your internal battery to get back in gear and ready to go for yet another round of teaching. Be good to yourself by picking and choosing from the following:

1. Take time each day to regroup—time to renew, relax, and re-fresh.
2. Be still and just listen. Listen to your inner spirit and reflect.
3. Create a happiness journal. Focus on what makes you happy and write about it.
4. Stand, stretch, and loosen up your muscles. Stretching will allevi-ate tension.
5. Breathe deeply and breathe deeply again. Slow down your breath-ing and relax.
6. Connect with nature. Observe the natural beauty that abounds and surrounds you.
7. Concentrate on one color and look for that color wherever you are. Really look for the greens, the blues, whatever your choice. You'll be surprised what you've overlooked.

8. Spend time at a nearby museum or art gallery. Appreciate the creative displays.
9. Listen to classical music; it builds a better brain.
10. Create a new recipe. Go ahead, experiment with eating something different.
11. Forget about the past, get over it, and concentrate on the future.
12. Take a walk around the block. Then go in a different direction.
13. Go fly a kite! Literally. Try it; it's fun. It's probably been years since you have.
14. Call a friend and thank them for their friendship.
15. Remember why you became a teacher. Rekindle the passion behind your decision.
16. Remind yourself that you are an effective teacher and that you are doing a good job.
17. Create a stress-free zone in your home or apartment—a place just for you. It doesn't have to be a big space—perhaps a hammock or lounge chair may be equipped with stereo headphones. Use it as a place to relax and unwind.

YOUR IDEAL LEVEL OF PERFORMANCE— BEING YOUR BEST

I am amazed at how similar our performance, as teachers, is when compared to the world of athletics and sports. Successful athletes realize the all-important connection between the mind and body. The "inside job" of maintaining the mental edge has become the singular advantage of winning athletes. The link between physical activities and mental states are apparent in the growing awareness and acceptance of the concept of visualization. Mental rehearsal and visualizing your performance is a beneficial process. In addition to the visual aspects of practicing in our mind's eye, positive self-talk and our innermost thoughts and attitudes come into play.

What does this mean for a teacher? Try this. In the space below, write a brief description of one of your best lessons.

_____

_____

_____

_____

_____

_____

_____

Remember that lesson when you were really on fire? The flow of your lesson was smooth. The words you used were clear, the responses to your student's questions were succinct, and the students' reactions were very positive and outstanding. As you were teaching that lesson, you could do no wrong. You were witty and alert. All the students were attentive and involved in the lesson. They were with you all the way. As you describe that lesson in the space above, do your best to recreate that scenario and all the right conditions. The point is that you performed excellently, and, chances are, you were in a zone. Many athletes refer to the zone as that situation when everything is going well and there is a smooth connection between the mental and physical. There is a feeling of being connected to one's inner being with all the conditions just right.

Another way of looking at your ideal level of performance is through the concept of being centered. The centered approach to performance can be compared to various practices of martial arts or Eastern philosophies. A centered approach is a state of being or a level of functioning where an individual is able to achieve and maintain a sense of heightened awareness that is free of tension and is enabled to act with purpose without being distracted. In a centered state, we are more conscious of our inner being, and there is a connection between the mind and body. This leads to an ability to truly focus on obtaining the results we want at that moment in time.

I first learned of this centered approach through associates who practice martial arts and yoga. During personal consultations, they have showed me the importance of being centered, to concentrate on our points of gravity, posture, and movement. We can actually enhance our presence and our readiness to perform by concentrating on our potential to be centered. It is an ideal state of peak performance in which we are more aware of our surroundings and sense of purpose. It is a way of accomplishing more without struggle, because we are functioning at a higher level of our being and using more of our potential. It also deals with our physical self, our body structure, and how we carry ourselves.

Focus on the midregion of your body to determine where your center of gravity is. This will help you to accomplish more of a positive connection between your muscular-skeletal systems and where your weight is distributed. The mid-region of the body, near the hips where the lower torso connects with the upper torso, is an important point of concentration. Understanding this sense of personal gravity can give you a greater awareness of your mind-body connection and can be a source of energy as you call upon your vast, untapped physical reserves.

If we really focus and concentrate on those past best performances, we will be able to re-create them in a present tense. The potential to be centered lies within us at all times. We also need to be more aware of our breathing, control our thoughts, regulate the images we hold in our mind, and initiate our self-talk. By being more aware of these matters, we can then re-create the centered approach of the optimal mind-body connection for a greater sense of purpose and to tap into the potential and talent that often lies dormant within ourselves.

This higher level of functioning can increase your performance at any given time. It begins with breathing. Deep breathing leads to a more centered state. Breathe deeply, slowly, and deliberately, and concentrate on your abdominal/stomach area. As you continue to breathe, clearly visualize yourself feeling more centered. It can reenergize you and allow you to be more fully aware of your surroundings and more in tune with your feelings. Then focus only on the elements and factors that are necessary for you to perform at your best with a greater sense of achievement and a higher level of accomplishment. Your thoughts become more positive and focused, and you are then able to see the powerful connection between the mind-body.

Your students will notice this transformation as well. They will be able to see you function efficiently and perform at your best. This increased peak performance in the classroom gives self-confidence and a greater belief in your abilities.

PHYSICAL FITNESS

> My doctor recently told me that jogging could add years to my life.
> I think he was right. I feel ten years older already.
>
> —Milton Berle

No doubt about it. Teaching places both mental and physical demands on you. In a typical day, you are stretched, pulled, tugged, and literally torn as you go about your activities. During a typical classroom period, you are processing many inputs of data. As you typically "stand and deliver," there are literally thousands of things occurring in your classroom. Within the four walls of your arena is a tremendous amount of activity. Classrooms are busy places, even during so-called structured lessons, and there are a variety of pockets of occurrences that are evolving.

Just imagine what goes on in a classroom of 28 students. Some students are actually paying attention. Those are the easy ones. Some are daydreaming or thinking about something very removed from what you're teaching. And others have no idea what is going on. They sit silently, not betraying their confusion or indifference. Upon observation, the class may appear to be with you. But on closer examination, many other things are actually going on. One student slips a personal note to another. One begins to doze off. A particularly mischievous boy tugs at the girl's hair in front of him. Several students raise their hands to ask questions. A nearly inaudible message barks from the intercom, and a potentially irate parent arrives early for an appointment.

It is quite exhausting processing all these activities. Throughout the day, our energy wanes, and we are not as sharp as we should be. We can also lose our edge because of all of the stress and constant interruptions. Just getting back to that student who is still waiting for an answer to a question asked over ten minutes ago takes a major shift of focus and places physical demands on you. In order to maintain our energy level and make it through the day, it is important to be and stay in good physical shape.

There are many reasons why people don't work-out—lack of time, poor planning, low self-image, the failure to see immediate benefits, lack of motivation, or the mistaken notion that exercise will make them tired. In reality, exercise actually energizes the body. Others claim that they don't know how to exercise or believe that they are not athletic and, therefore, avoid exercise. Many teachers I know tend to say, "I'm too tired to exercise." Actually, I believe that if you say you are too tired to exercise, then you are probably tired because you don't exercise.

Well, if you are into daily exercise, congratulations! You are well aware of the many benefits of exercise. If you are into exercising less frequently, say three or four times per week, that's wonderful, too. Most experts on physical fitness recommend at least three or four days of planned exercise per week.

For years, recommendations were prevalent that the real benefit of exercise occurred only after a sustained period of time of, say, at least 20 minutes. That, I believe has swayed many people away from developing an exercise program. Some people were convinced that a 20-minute period of time devoted to exercise might not have been manageable in their busy schedules. Now, experts on physical fitness and exercise recommend an accumulation of time devoted to activity, which is more of a collective sum of exertion done over a period of time.

In other words, there are still benefits from exercise and physical activity and movement acquired over a period of time. Time spent in doing physical activity rather than remaining sedentary contributes to your total exercise time. If you accumulate exercise time in smaller increments, you can start a realistic regimen in no time. For instance, if you park your car further away from your actual destination and walk, that extra walk time can be a part of your total time. If you choose to take the steps rather than the elevator, that, too, is advantageous and can be a part of the total. If you walk around your school building or in the halls rather than just staying in your classroom, that walk time is a part of your grand total.

I highly recommend one of two approaches to increase your amount of physical activity. Either increase your overall physical movement and exertion by accumulating time or actually devote a portion of each day (or at least four days per week) to a planned exercise program.

In my own life, I have always made it a point to exercise. During one of my relocations, one of the very first things I did was to join a local health club. Even before I found employment, shortly after I moved, I scouted out the area health clubs and exercise facilities. Within one day of my arrival, I joined a health club and made it a point to go on a regular basis.

During all those years at the club, I have noticed a small group of individuals who are still exercising on a regular basis. This group of regulars has remained trim and fit. They are full of energy and vitality. They really have a zest for living. These people have been my inspiration to continue using the facility. They look better, have more enthusiasm, and stay healthier. In fact, there is a group of members who are in their 70s and 80s who still exercise together.

In contrast, every January, many new members join the club. New Year's resolutions and holiday gift memberships bring many new faces to the facility. It has become a disappointing ritual. These well-meaning people hope to incorporate an exercise program into their lives, but something happens. Most of those new memberships last only about three weeks and then they drop out. They quit before the behavior becomes fixed in their daily routine; moreover, they quit before they actually experience any benefits from the exercise. With no immediate results, they walked away from developing a routine that would allow them to continue.

How unfortunate. If only they would have continued for at least 28 to 30 days. Then they may have persisted. Why do I say 28 to 30 days? Well, think about it. That seems to be the standard staying time required for rehab programs and treatment facilities where people go for various kinds of addictions. The human psyche needs that period of time for old habits to be broken down and new habits to be acquired.

I recommend a balanced combination of both aerobic and anaerobic activities. Aerobic-type activities require greater amounts of oxygen and include walking, swimming, biking, running, dancing, tennis, racquetball, and calisthenics. Anaerobic activities do not have the same oxygen requirements. Weight lifting is a good example where more oxygen is not needed.

Through aerobic exercises, we strengthen the heart muscle. The heart muscle becomes stronger because of the need to pump more oxygen-rich blood in and out of the heart. Weight lifting is more beneficial to the muscular, skeletal system and enhances posture and joint functions. Both types of exercise, of course, are advantageous. Some of the many benefits include:

- Helps limit weight gain
- Increases in stamina and energy

- Reduces blood pressure
- Enhances sleep
- Strengthens our immune system
- Helps to maintain bone structure and offset brittle bones
- Improves blood sugar control in diabetes
- Helps reduce arthritic pain
- Improves our endurance levels, flexibility, and balance
- Helps avoid injury
- Helps in handling stress and eases tension
- Offsets depression and decreases anxiety

In terms of your profession, think about how much more effective you could be in your daily teaching activities if you were in better shape. As you well know, teaching makes both mental and physical demands. In addition to staying mentally alert, it is important to have the physical stamina and endurance to make it through each day of teaching. In many respects, the school year can be viewed as a marathon, your own personal marathon to make it through your academic year. On typical days, you can go home nearly exhausted. I do want to acknowledge that. As your school day comes to a close, you are drained and probably wondering, "How on earth could I possibly exercise? I'm too tired to exercise!"

I know many teachers who go to an exercise facility immediately after school. This planned activity devoted exclusively to yourself can be very beneficial. By exercising at the end of your day, you can release all of the stress and tension that has built up. It can actually loosen you up, clear your mind, and give you a refreshing perspective—yes, even peace of mind. It adds to a more calm and tranquil feeling and helps you handle stress more effectively. When you get home, you'll feel more invigorated, a little tired, yes, but ready to finish your evening activities. Remember, you still have household chores, family matters, and, yes, papers to grade. That daily exercise might be just the transition you need to separate work from personal life.

On the other hand, you may prefer to exercise before going to school. In this way, you'll be able to build up a reserve of energy, a positive, go-for-it attitude and the luxury of knowing that you have already accomplished one goal before most of your peers and students have even started their days. This too, can be very beneficial, especially if you are an early riser. Other options include breaking up your exercise, doing part in the morning, part after work. Think about your own metabolism and natural rhythms and preferences, and then schedule your exercise regimen. Tie this into your daily planning and time management schedules.

I highly encourage you to get into the habit of regular, daily exercise as soon as possible. If you can't exercise every day, as little as four days per week would be a suitable goal. As a supplement to formal exercise, look for ways to maximize your physical exertion in your daily activities and endeavors. For instance, I have developed a set of abdominal exercises that I routinely use while driving long distances in my car. Safety, attention, and following of all road rules and regulations are paramount, but while driving, why not do some stomach work, like isometrics, stomach crunches, and toning-type movements?

Also, as you run errands and go about your daily routine, look for ways to gain some extra physical exertion. Parking further away from your destination might add a few minutes to your commute or local trips, but the total time of that activity adds to your cumulative exercise. Even while I am going to the health club to work out, I always make it a point to park far away from the main entrance. The extra walking distance adds up to more exertion.

PARKING LOT PARADOX

The health club parking lot is often an amusing place. Most people drive around looking for the closest space to the main entrance. I have observed people to even stop and wait for a spot to open up, just to be near the doors. These same people then think nothing of using the treadmill for 45 minutes to an hour. I have even witnessed both verbal and physical altercations and disputes occur over who had the parking space first. Once, after seeing two patrons nearly come to blows over a parking space, I noticed later, that both were on treadmills for over 45 minutes. Rather than getting agitated, worked up, and upset over a parking space, their exercise routine could have been more effective, their blood pressure reduced, and their attitudes more serene simply by not arguing over a parking space and walking a bit further to enter the building. After all, they were going inside to exercise and work up a sweat anyway.

Our lifestyle choices certainly impact our individual longevity. How well we age is often determined more by what we do than who we are genetically. The aging process seems to depend on our lifestyle, our choices, and our behavior. Research supports the importance of eating properly, remaining physically fit, staying mentally challenged, building a support system, and doing all we can to stay independent as possible.

GETTING STARTED

If you have never exercised or find yourself not sticking with a routine, then I urge you to try this approach. Prior to actually working out is a period of time when we think about exercising, contemplate going to an exercise facility, or freeing up some time to devote to an exercise. This period of time is sort of a mental debate. We wonder if we should work out, and we decide if we can actually devote the time to a session. The preworkout self-talk goes something like this: "Are you sure you want to do this?" "Yes, exercise is good for me." "Sure, but you're *sooo* tired, you don't have the time, and you can't find your cross-training shoes." That is the worst kind of self-doubt. Before you know it, you've talked yourself out of working out.

We know that if we can just begin exercising, we'll feel better afterward. And, we'll be glad that we did. It's actually getting started that is so difficult. The major difference between people who get fit and stay fit and those who do not is the ability to win the preexercise self-talk mental dialogue. By not listening to those excuses and driving by your workout facility instead of driving into the parking lot and using the facility, you will benefit by all the rewards that come with regular exercise.

Winning the mental debate is a skill that you can master. Through desire, you can overcome the self-doubts and take action. The more you decide to avoid these pitfalls, the more it empowers you to be action-oriented and in charge of your life.

It is also a good idea to distinguish between mental exhaustion versus physical exhaustion. After a long day of teaching, you understandably feel exhausted. Often it is more mental than physical—a mental state that feels like a lack of energy. This may lead us to avoid any physical activity whatsoever, but once you get your body moving, you soon become physically energized.

Throughout your teaching day, prepare your body by eating well. I find it better to eat high-protein, low-carbohydrate kinds of snacks. And it is essential to consume plenty of water. Staying well-hydrated throughout the day benefits the brain. In addition, water helps maintain our vocal cords, which, of course, are vital to the teaching profession. Eating properly and consuming plenty of water keeps blood sugar steady and increases energy levels. The more energetic you feel, the more you are likely to engage in and stick to a fitness regime.

So, the next time you find yourself debating whether you should head to the gym, remove those doubts, stay motivated, and establish the momentum necessary to start and complete that workout. Once your body takes over and you begin exercising, you will be glad you did. Those excuses will fade away and your forward motion will prevail.

Once you've won that battle, the next hurdle will be maintaining an ongoing, systematic, and continuous level of motivation to persevere and making regular exercise a daily habit in your lifestyle. For most new exercisers, it's much easier to just quit than it is to get and stay fit. Finding the will to stick with a program can be a difficult struggle.

It's a shame that many who adopt an exercise program quit within a very short period of time. Those who stick with exercise programs have managed to make their workout routines an important part of their personal identity. A common problem for the quitters is that they did not overcome the initial phase of discomfort and pain to get to the point where the benefits of exercise kick in. It's in that magical moment when we get by that discomfort, go beyond the aches and pains, and experience the real enjoyment of fitness. That feeling of extreme satisfaction comes only after a period of adjustment. So find an enjoyable, satisfying activity and stick with it. Keep doing it until it becomes a habit. At that moment, you will then begin to really experience the joy and fulfillment of exercise. So stay positive, set goals, build confidence in yourself, and realize that you can do it.

DIET

"Eat, Drink and Be Merry . . . For Tomorrow We Diet"

"Oh no," you might say, "not another treatise on dieting!" Dieting, unfortunately, has become both a national obsession and one of our collective failures. We spend thousands on books, fat-free prepared meals, packaged diet plans, and questionable capsules with vague organic ingredients, yet we are still overweight and out of shape. Well, it is inevitable that if I am going to include physical fitness as an important aspect to your development as a teacher, we have to take a look at diet, too.

When I entered my fourth decade of life, I began to notice various changes in terms of weight, appearance, energy, and general attitude. Now, I had been careful to not buy into that old stereotype of being over the hill; yet, I did notice that weight went on much easier than ever before, but went off much more slowly and with greater difficulty than ever before. Therefore, as I found myself having to adjust my belt and buying larger pants, I decided to take some action and offset the effects of maturity I was experiencing.

As I mentioned, in my early 40s, I began to experience and sense a different type of reaction to the foods I ate and the amount of intake. In previous years, I was able to make quick adjustments and slight modifications so my desired weight would once again easily be achieved. However, by the age of 42, I noticed that the things I did before to lose weight did not work. For instance, in the spring, I would usually go on a diet for about six weeks and, low and behold, my weight would be right back to where it should be. Like others, I had a habit of really enjoying myself the last two months of each year. With all the various traditional social, religious, and festive seasonal gatherings during November and December, I would really take advantage of the availability of food at many celebrations.

Well, the usual adjustments that I would make during my six-week maintenance diet, for the first time, did not work. I had lost nothing—a big zero! Well, that sent a message to me that I had to go back to the drawing board and redesign a better way of maintaining my desired weight. In my case, I carefully began to monitor the types of food I ate, calculate the amounts, and note the combinations of foods. What I found out through this awareness phase of really examining my diet was that I had relied a great deal on the usual items I would buy and have on-hand to eat. Things like bread, bagels, bananas, potatoes, rice, and corn comprised a major part of my overall diet. This close monitoring process was very helpful to me.

Then, I thoroughly studied and reviewed three very popular, mainstream, bestsellers on diets, and compared and contrasted the features and benefits of each one. My review of these popular diets led to an important discovery. Most of the types of foods that were mainstays in my diet were not recommended in any these three books. The authors of these best-selling diet books all shared one common opinion. They stressed that foods like bagels (especially nonwheat ones), white bread, bananas, corn, rice, carrots, pretzels, potato chips, potatoes, pasta, and, of course, most desserts were thought to be detrimental to the weight loss programs that they were promoting. So that day, as I completed my review, I decided to eliminate those foods for six weeks. I was surprised to see that during that short time, I lost 23 pounds. More importantly, my weight was reduced in such a way that it was virtually painless. And my weight distribution was perfect. I lost inches in my waist, but maintained the definition in my muscles. With the exception of eliminating the listed foods, I ate just about everything else that I wanted to and in whatever amounts I desired. I took no note of my total consumption. I ate until I was satisfied. (Remember to pause at various points of the meal to let your brain receive the signals from the stomach.) All I did was just eliminate those foods high in grain content (carbohydrates) that all three books agreed with.

In addition, I reviewed the authors' recommendations and compared them to my lifestyle, considering whether it was practical or feasible for me. Those recommendations that fit my lifestyle I adopted; those that didn't, I rejected. I knew that the choice was mine. It was totally up to me. After those six weeks, I decided to not eat those types of foods. I eliminated all of them from my diet, with the exception of desserts! I feel that if we use our discretion and control ourselves, then we can enjoy desserts and other sweet delicacies in moderation. You might choose another personal indulgence. Desserts happened to be mine.

In order to compensate for my need to stay at my desired weight and still have my sweets, I then tried another angle in my own personal diet plan. For my purposes, it has worked wonders. For the past four years, I have been able to eat most foods (having eliminated breads, potatoes, carrots, rice, and corn) with no consideration of how much else I eat.

There are the rare occasions I have little or no choice, such as at a banquet or a precatered dinner. Still, I maintain a level of moderation that allows me to enjoy the food and not experience any guilt or weight gain.

In order to still enjoy my favorite desserts, such as cake, ice cream, and pastries, I have created a plan that has worked wonders for me. I call my approach the "Off Again-On Again 5/2 Diet." I now eat sweets and desserts only on Saturdays and Sundays. Monday through Friday, I avoid them as much as possible (it is easy). And I eat just about anything else. Initially, it's difficult to pass up that doughnut with the morning coffee, but once the habit is established, there is no sense of craving. Since the incorporation of this 5/2 plan, I have not gained any weight. What I have gained is a better sense of discipline as I wait for my rewards, my yummy desserts on weekends. I have also gained better control over what types of food I eat. The beneficial inclusion of many fresh fruits and vegetables are now the mainstay of my daily diet. The concentration of fruits and vegetables has led to increased energy, more alertness, a better feeling, and a sense of appreciation for the mind-body-diet connection.

Earlier, I stressed that you do not need this book to decide what your ideal weight is or what type of diet you should choose. All I am saying is that this approach has worked miracles for me. You decide what is best for you and determine how you can best achieve it. I have found that I am very much a self-directed type of person. If I need some information, I will obtain it. If I need to lose weight, I will do it. If I need to eliminate a habit, then I will stop that type of behavior. You may not be as self-directed, so this information is presented as a model to practice, adapt, accept, or reject. Still, I am quite amazed how well the on-again, off-again approach has worked for me. Try your own approach, just for the sake of research.

Now, what about those inevitable snack cravings and the need for quick energy in a pinch? In addition to a heavy reliance on fruits and vegetables, I also include nuts like walnuts, pistachios, hazelnuts, almonds, and cashews. These types of nuts not only are nutritious, they also have the beneficial type of cholesterol that you keep reading about. They also offer a quick burst of protein that substitutes for the sugar-buzz that many of us crave early in the afternoon when our blood sugar levels are low. You can eat nuts to ward off that sleepy, fatigued feeling right after lunch (and after all, that feeling is already reduced by your diet adjustments and exercise regimen). You might never have to buy candy bars again. I feel that it is vitally important to develop an actual plan of action that includes a firm date for the beginning of your diet plan. Once you plan it, and pick that target date, go for it! Stick with it and don't stop until you have reached your goal. Then keep on going.

Personally, I do not believe in the food pyramid approach to diet and nutrition. In my opinion, the recommendations found in the Food Guide Pyramid have done more harm than good. I feel that it is scientifically unfounded advice that misleads a lot of individuals. It tends to put too much emphasis on red meat, and groups together too many different types of carbohydrates. It is my contention that there should be more emphasis placed on fruits, vegetables, nuts, fish, and poultry.

I encourage you to take a closer look at the pyramid and what it means to you and your choice of food and also to the types of carbohydrates that you consume. Please study the differences between the types of fats, especially the ones that are good for your heart. As you monitor your own diet habits and compare what is best for you, you can then be better able to determine which foods protect you against diseases, keep your digestive tract in better shape, keep your hunger at bay, and suppress your appetite.

I enjoy a regular consumption of nuts, which I used in my diet to break old habits of potato chips and pretzels. By replacing empty calorie type snacks with more nutritious nuts, there are many benefits because nuts contain fiber, minerals, vitamins, and the healthy unsaturated fats.

Having made those conscious decisions earlier has now paid off as I entered the fifth decade of my life. I made a concentrated effort to study diet, nutrition, food groupings, and the body's reaction to certain types of food. We will look at the connection that diet and nutrition have on your ability to be the best teacher possible. I believe that we can teach better and be more effective if we feel good, look great, and are physically and mentally ready to perform in our roles as educators. As you know, there is sound relevancy in the mind-body connection.

I urge you to look at ways to better your overall health, develop a heightened feeling of well-being, boost your energy level, and increase your stamina. All this has a direct link to your outlook on life and your perspective on teaching. I'm sure your mother told you time and again to eat fruits and vegetables every day. Now, we see various reports and research findings on the many benefits of these kinds of diets. It's still a bit surprising that old maternal advice and modern scientific research have come to the same conclusions.

Give it a try. Starting tomorrow, begin to add more fresh fruit and a variety of vegetables to your present diet, and you, too, will begin to feel better, look better, and gain new levels of energy. Also, I urge you to do your own review of recent nutritional reports on healthy ways to eat. You really don't need a book to make you aware. You know it already. You probably just need to develop a plan of action.

By reviewing the research on your own (like you would encourage your students to do), you will see that fruits, like blueberries and straw-berries, deliver a high level of disease fighting antioxidants. Antioxidants seem to have a major role in the prevention of and/or delay of the onset of life-threatening diseases, such as cancer and heart disease. They have also been found to be beneficial in slowing the aging process. Plus, they contain a number of substances that are recognized to have other sig-nificant health benefits. Substances in fruits and vegetables also assist us in our response to stress and help to improve our balance and physical coordination. And they taste good.

If your current weight is an issue with you, then I urge you to care-fully examine what and how much you eat, and then make a decision to do something about it. If you need and want to lose weight, then it is en-tirely up to you. You certainly don't need this book to decide. Remem-ber, however, that a major part of the decision to become a teacher was to help others improve their lives. You certainly can be more efficient in this process if you practice what you teach!

Above all, I encourage you to decide what is best for yourself. This book is not intended to answer all of your questions about diet and nu-trition. I only offer some ideas as a means of getting you to think about these important matters. As I have thoroughly reviewed many famous diet plans and programs as well as scientific studies, there tends to be a general agreement emerge: fruits, vegetables, grains, and nuts are good for you and should be the foundation of a healthy diet. Ultimately, it is up to you to decide.

I am convinced of this though; for increased energy and endurance necessary to teach in today's schools, your diet is important. For instance, next time you get those cravings for something sweet, like a candy-bar, try replacing the white-sugar sweet with some nuts. Nuts, like almonds, walnuts, and cashews, can give you a burst of energy and sustain your stamina.

TAKE CARE OF YOUR VOICE

Teachers fall into the same category as actors, singers, stand-up comedians, broadcasters, corporate trainers, athletic coaches, and other performers. All of these professions rely on their vocal cords in order to do their jobs.

Since teaching depends so much on the voice, it would be very difficult, if not impossible, to be an effective teacher without it. You know how difficult it is to do your job on those days when your voice is not up to par. Throat irritations, colds, hay fever, and laryngitis all affect the quality of your voice. Overuse of your vocal cords can result in pain, discomfort, and poor vocal quality.

I recommend that you start to be kinder to your voice. I believe that teachers need to consider the voice as a necessary, vital, and essential part of their livelihood. Think of the following occupations and the associated tool of the trade:

- A carpenter and his saw
- An auto repair technician and her wrench
- A doctor and his stethoscope
- A police officer and hand-cuffs
- A chef and her carving knife
- A quarterback and his football
- A computer programmer and her software
- A landscaper and his lawn mower

I'm sure you get the point. These professions would be severely hampered by the lack of even one of those tools or resources. As educators, you need your vocal cords to be ready and able to function. Even if you don't have a chalk/white-board, a computer, or even a text, your voice can deliver the lesson. But without a well-maintained voice, your effectiveness as a teacher is diminished greatly.

The more you view your voice as a necessity, the more you will realize how important it is to be kinder to your vocal cords. Fortunately, there is a growing trend to equip classrooms with voice amplification systems. If you teach in one of the schools or districts that recognizes the importance of microphones and speakers in the classroom, then that's terrific. You are very fortunate to be associated with such a school system. More and more schools now have amplified classrooms not only to save the teachers voice from strain and overuse, but also to better ensure that all students can adequately hear. Schools that have equipped their classrooms with voice amplification systems have reported many benefits. Students pay better attention, are more alert, and are more likely to be well-behaved. Teaching is more efficient.

I have learned about this issue personally several years ago. I was experiencing some persistent and reoccurring voice irritation and strain. Realizing just how important my voice was to my teaching, I made an appointment at a well-known university's voice center. Although I realized the importance of my voice, unfortunately, my health insurance provider did not. The cost of treatment amounted to several thousands of dollars, but my local HMO rejected my request and blatantly told me that voice treatments were not necessary and that the costs would not be covered.

I know we are living in an era of radical healthcare reform and medical coverage for questionable procedures has become a national issue; yet, I was extremely disappointed with the cavalier and flippant reason given for the denial. Consequently, I appealed the denial and found that I had to justify and substantiate why it was necessary to receive the voice treatments. My main argument was that my voice was vital to my livelihood and that I relied on it much like an athlete relies on certain parts of the body to perform. During my appeal, I compared the voice of an educator to the knee joint of the carpet layer—both essential. I asked if they would deny knee treatments to a carpet installer or reject hand/finger treatments to a professional piano player. Suddenly, they started to get my point. Through that convincing argument, I was finally able to have my claim approved. As a result of that experience, I was able to learn some expert methods, techniques, and strategies that have enabled me to take better care of my voice.

These suggestions are based on established practices and recommendations of experts. Try them and you can better save, restore, and maintain your valuable voice.

1. Start to look at your vocal cords much like you would do other body parts, like joints or muscles. Realize that the vocal cords can be damaged or injured much like other parts of our bodies.

2. It is important to "warm-up" the vocal cord area, just like we would do before a workout or exercise routine.

3. Breathing is important. Just like singers or stage actors breathing properly allows us to take in sufficient air to speak long phrases without losing volume and projection. Breathe from the diaphragm, the large muscle just below the ribcage.

4. Stay hydrated. Drink plenty of water.

5. Avoid clearing your throat or coughing prior to or while you are speaking. The usual way of clearing your throat is actually damaging, especially the traditional combination of cough and sound effect. It actually causes further strain and stress to the vocal cords. Instead, get in the habit of opening your vocal cords by inhaling and exhaling a flow of air (silently) over your vocal cords. In other words, you may want to simulate a yawn and concentrate on opening the air passage through your mouth, and then gently inhale and exhale a flow of air that can glide over your vocal cords.

6. Use your hand to massage your throat area. Take your hand, palm facing you, and in the area between your thumb and forefinger, place it on your throat. In a gentle fashion, rub your hand over your throat below your chin and to the area where your neck meets your shoulder/chest area. Gently glide your hand back and forth, while actually massaging the vocal chord area. This will warm-up and loosen your vocal cords. Do this several times throughout the day. (You may want to do this warm-up technique in private, as it may look strange to someone who doesn't know why you're doing it.) Perhaps you may want to include this ritual in your commute, while waiting at traffic lights or in stop-and-go traffic. It might confuse other drivers who see you, but you'll have a warmed-up voice before you hit the classroom. Just remember to drive safely!

7. As a warm-up, do exaggerated facial movements as you enunciate certain words or phrases. For instance, I repeatedly say, "He is home" as one of my routines. I say very slowly and enunciate very

dramatically each word. As I say he, I extend the sound like, "he-e-e-e-e-e-e-e-e" to a full breath and "is-s-s-s-s-s-s-s" to another full breath and say "home" fully and distinctly for another extended breath. I have also found that saying, "king kong, ding dong" several times in much the same way, is another good warm-up. These nonsense phrases are effective as a means of concentrating on saying the words slowly and using extended lip movements.

8. In addition to massaging the vocal cords, I recommend that you concentrate on rubbing your jaw areas. One effective way is to use both hands to massage the cheek and jaw bones. Here's how it works. With both hands, make a fist and place each fist on your cheekbones. Now with your closed fist in the knuckle area, gently rotate your hands as you rub your cheekbones. Concentrate on the full area of the side of your face. In a gently rotating fashion, loosen up your jaw area. In a small circular fashion, massage the joints of your jaw. This should invigorate that area and energize you to project your voice better. This is similar to a track athlete stretching a leg muscle prior to a race.

9. In the area directly below your chin take your hand and put your thumb on the knuckle joint of your forefinger, then place your hand with the thumb below your chin, and place the knuckle of your forefinger in front of your chin. This then becomes the position for an isometric kind of warm-up. With your hand, apply some pressure while opening and closing your mouth. This kind of resistance is another way to make better use of the delivery of your voice.

10. Walk before you talk. Let me describe this one further. In the comfort of our homes, communication occurs in many different locations. To better preserve your voice, avoid overextending your volume when it's really not necessary to project your voice. For example, in our two-story home, it is very common for my wife and I to try to talk to each other while each is on a different floor. You know what I mean, you are upstairs and your partner is downstairs and says, "Honey, have you seen my (insert favorite misplaced item)?" Before you shout out a response, walk before you talk. Rather than shouting out loud in a raised voice that will

only strain your vocal cords, walk closer to where your partner is and then answer the question in a normal tone of voice. This will not only save your voice from overuse, it will also be more advantageous as a means getting some beneficial exercise and movement. And, who knows? You might enhance your relationship at the same time.

After a long day of teaching, you may find that your voice tires more easily and you even may be in some pain associated with speaking. Perhaps you have found that your voice even sounds rough and gravelly more often. If that is the case with you, then you probably need to take better care of your voice.

One of the common causes of a tired voice is, of course, overuse. There's nothing at all startling with that assessment. Yet in addition to overuse, other probable causes can contribute to voice problems. Most likely poor breathing habits, muscle tension in the neck and throat areas, as well as overstraining are factors you should be concerned with. Muscle tension can be the result of general strain, poor vocal techniques, and the high demands placed on your vocal chords.

Excessive talking, too much throat clearing, shouting, inefficient breathing patterns, anxiety, emotional stress, and physical fatigue are all common causes leading to vocal abuse. Sometimes, a bit of a rest period, maybe over a weekend, or even a day off, is all that you may need to help your voice recover. However, at other times you may need more of an ongoing plan of action to ensure that your voice stays in shape.

If your voice is mildly strained, you can usually rest it and it will bounce back. Yet, to avoid overusing it again, it is advisable to always be sure to properly warm-up your voice. A short period of controlled, soft vocal exercises can help you to keep your voice in better shape. Some gentle scales, much like a singer uses, can limber-up your vocal chords. Also, learn to breathe properly through your nose and mouth and deep into the recesses of your lungs and stomach area. Your voice will respond better. Even humming a favorite tune can get your vocal chords ready to respond.

In addition to the warm-ups, breathing, and rest periods, think of other ways that you can actually save your voice. In what ways can you avoid overusing of your voice? First, do you always have to shout? Can just a few words suffice, rather than a long-winded answer to a question? How about standing or sitting closer to the person you want to talk to. Instead of yelling down the hall or across the room, just get closer to the person you want to talk to.

Another important consideration is to be more aware of your posture while speaking to your class. Avoid being hunched over or crossing your arms. Maintain an erect posture and be more open with your arms and hand gestures. Watch out for muscle tension and make the necessary adjustments like massaging your throat and jaw areas or deep breathing as a means to loosen up.

8

YOU'RE NEVER TOO OLD TO TEACH

I have seen some amazing trends arise in teaching. On one hand, I have witnessed a sort of exodus, large groups of teachers leaving the profession who are only in their early to mid-50s, whereas on the other, there is a group of second-career people who are just entering the field in their 40s and 50s.

I often wonder what makes a person who chose teaching as a career earlier in life suddenly take the first available retirement option. I also ponder the logic of other professionals who, after becoming successful in one discipline, change directions entirely and enter education. I have a hunch that some of the early departures may have had enough; yet, I believe that in many cases, they are being pushed out, as if there is some sort of notion that they are too old to teach. Successful teachers come in all shapes, sizes, and ages. And I have felt that the teacher's age is really a neutral factor. A good teacher always keeps up with the latest trends. What I am addressing here is that some teachers may have a mistaken notion that they are simply too old to teach. I have heard many remarks comparing veteran teachers with recent college graduates and teachers new to the profession, and, all too often, these comparisons are between which group is better prepared to teach.

I read an article many years ago that continues to provide me with a great deal of inspiration. The headline read:

"At 96, Prof. Teaches on in Good Humor"

Since the day I discovered this article, I have kept it prominently on display. It has become a source of motivation for me as Professor Abe Goldstein continued to teach even at the age of 96.

Another tremendously illustrative example is the 81-year-old substitute teacher, Arnold Blume, who remains very active and on-call to report to the Great Neck North Middle School in Great Neck, New York. Experience Works is a nonprofit organization based in Arlington, Virginia, that provides job training and placement services for senior citizens and lobbies on their behalf.

Keep Arnold Blume in mind as you drive to your next day of teaching. Keep him in mind on Sunday night as you dread returning to your classroom on Monday and begin another week. I know that it is easy to have self-doubt and feelings of frustration at times. Many teachers wonder if it's all worth it. My answer is always, "Yes, indeed it is."

Maintaining a career long after most persons retire is becoming more and more common, so even if you don't remain on the job into your triple-digits, you can still derive inspiration and realize that age does not have to mean limitations.

In the world of sports, there are many examples of coaches who do not listen to age-related barriers or stigmas. The legendary coaches of the 2006 Orange Bowl are perfect examples of age having no boundaries. In a classic match-up between the two most-winning coaches in college football history, Bobby Bowden of Florida State University and Joe Paterno of Penn State University led their teams into national prominence, as they competed in a major bowl game. Paterno continues to coach at the age of 80, and the 77-year-old Bowden is still at the helm. These patriarchs of college football serve as successful role models. Keep these people in mind if you have thoughts that maybe you are too old to teach.

No doubt, teaching is a very demanding and taxing profession. More and more, teachers are reporting feeling burned-out and exhausted. At times, you may think that time has passed you by and that maybe you are not as effective as you once were. We all have those periods of doubt and despair. The next time you think that you're ready to pack it all in, reread this chapter and regain some inspiration from the individuals who have stuck with their endeavors, have persevered and excelled, even at advanced ages to reach their next level of performance.

I am convinced that anyone can work well past retirement if they truly love what they are doing. But what if you are not even close to retirement, yet you still feel that your life and career haven't been what you expected or didn't turn out like you had planned? Some of the following examples might help you reconsider.

One of my favorite personalities is musician Carlos Santana. During the late 1960s and early 1970s, he fronted one of my favorite musical groups, Santana. Little did I know then that Carlos would not establish himself with prominence until February 23, 2000, when he won eight Grammy Awards, including album of the year for his "Supernatural" release. That night, he tied Michael Jackson's 1983 record for the most Grammy trophies in a single night. In addition, he won the "Best Album" honors at the American Music Awards gathering on January 17, 2000.

Talk about perseverance and dedication—to reappear with such gusto and to stick with something for over 30 years is impressive. Santana's hit song *Smooth* monopolized the radio airwaves as it held on to the number-one spot for over 16 weeks. That was quite a comeback and placed the guitarist high on the pedestal of success and at the top of the charts for the first time in a 30+-year career.

On the night of the American Music Awards, 52-year-old Santana was quoted as saying:

> A lot of people told me they didn't want to work with me because I'm old. Mr. Davis [Clive Davis of Arista Records] believed in me. We both believed we had a masterpiece in our belly.[12]

So what masterpiece do you still have within you? Remember that age has no bearing on excellence—in teaching, the music business, or any other endeavor you might have. What masterpiece are you still composing? What are your plans and aspirations? What unfinished business do you have that you are still working on? If Carlos Santana can achieve his greatest moment after over 30 years in the music industry, what can you do in your career as a teacher?

Lately, I have been hearing too many examples of age being a consideration in early retirements. Some recent college graduates tend to think that they have learned all of the latest techniques and they sometimes make disparaging remarks about the senior members of the faculty. My point is that we need to avoid stereotypes of age, regardless of your present age or level of experience. If you have something of value to offer, you can deliver your masterpiece of inspiration to your students.

If Santana and other musicians can still produce number-one songs, why can't teachers continue to create lesson plans and be successful in the classroom regardless of age? We are constantly reminded that age has no bearing on effective teaching, creativity, ingenuity, hard work, and initiative. Avoid labeling yourself or others according to any factors that really don't matter anyway. Good work and good teaching are timeless and cross all age groups.

Almost every motivational speaker likes to cite examples of persons who failed early in life but went on to major successes. I always like to point out to teachers, administrators, other professionals, and my students that two dominant figures of the American Civil War—namely Abraham Lincoln and his winning general Ulysses S. Grant—both failed miserably in their younger lives. Ray Kroc (of McDonald's fame), "Colonel" Harland Sanders (KFC), and Sam Walton (WalMart) were well into their senior years before they realized their life-long dreams of success and fortune.

THOUGHTS ABOUT LONGEVITY AND THE AGING PROCESS

I am fascinated by the number of people who live to be 100 years old. According to the latest census data, there are more persons over 100 in the country today than ever before. In fact, it's the fastest growing age cohort.

All too often, the aging process is filled with distortions, misconceptions, and negative expectations. It seems to me that, for many people, the power of expectations plays an important role in how they age. It is common to view the aging process as one that we have little or no control over. Granted, time stands still for no one and each day ticks away. We celebrate yet another milestone on our birthday. No, we can't stop time and birthdays, but I believe we can foster better expectations, more optimistic viewpoints, and positive attitudes about growing older.

Today, many teachers participate in retirement plans that are unique to their profession. Most public school systems are more than likely part of a statewide system, in which retirement programs tend to feature more benefits and lucrative payments than small companies or single employers. You may find yourself taking advantage of the "30-and-out" offer and retire in your early 50s. You want to be able to take full advantage of the retirement plan that your district or state offers you. It would be a shame if you were unable to really enjoy the fruits of your labor after your formal retirement. So, now is the time to begin to take better care of yourself today for a better tomorrow.

As you invest in your retirement pensions and other financial planning programs that you may have, remember that you need to include more than just the monetary deposits into those accounts. Look at yourself more holistically. The better you take care of yourself today physically, emotionally, and mentally, the more you will be able to enjoy those retirement years.

I believe that a lot of how we age depends on our lifestyles and choices that we make. Primarily, I am referring to your feelings about the process of aging. Are you optimistic or pessimistic? Do you look forward to your retirement days or do you dread getting older? Many people expect that as they age, they will get tired faster and feel stiff and sore more often—as if they almost expect to deteriorate. Our expectations and what we anticipate to happen to us are powerful parts of the end results we achieve.

I recommend that, instead, you view getting older as a new adventure, a time for renewal, and as an opportunity to gain new insights. Remove the stereotypes about the aging process that are detrimental. Look forward to tomorrow with a positive attitude and maintain a vision of yourself as staying well, having energy, and being able to function effectively. Get rid of those expectations that your health is only going to deteriorate. Expect the best, not the worst.

I am not naïve in disregarding the biological and physiological changes that occur in human beings as they age, but what I am specifically referring to is our attitudes, our viewpoints, and our thinking processes regarding longevity. We will be better off if we approach our older years with more optimism, and welcome it as a chance for a new endeavor in our lives and as an opportunity to continue living with enthusiasm. Welcome your future with the anticipation that you will feel fine, you will stay healthy, and you will be able to do the things you've been wanting to do all your life.

First, look for role models, people who have aged successfully. Tune into the birthday salutes, the kind that Willard Scott used to provide each morning. Convince yourself that if they can do it, so can you. One of my goals is to live to be at least 100. Expect that you, too, will be a part of the 100 club.

Recently, while traveling, I visited a toy museum. I had the privilege of being given a tour by a volunteer guide who proudly announced that she had just turned 81 years old. I told her that she was a true inspiration, and she proclaimed, "Growing old is all about attitude and having a positive attitude towards life." Her energy and zest for living really motivated me and convinced me even more that we can, to a great extent, control our own longevity.

An optimistic, positive outlook can increase the likelihood that we can age more gracefully. Optimists are not only happier; they are also healthier. I encourage you to do your own review of the literature to see just what the latest research has to say about the importance of having a positive mental attitude. Time and time again, studies about the lifestyles of people who live to be 100, all tend to identify positive thinking as one of the main factors that influence the aging process. Positive thinkers, experts believe, tend to be better at managing the strains of living and, thus, lower the levels of stress hormones. This process can enhance one's ability to withstand the pressures of living. The physical and mental challenges of aging can be better dealt with through a more optimistic frame of mind.

In addition to optimism, having a sense of humor is also an important factor. It is in your best interest to explore the connection between positive aging and humor. The benefits of laughter are no joke!

It is becoming more and more well-known that negative thinking and emotional distress are detrimental to our health. Humor can offer a way of intervening and offsetting the adverse conditions that we often face. By cultivating and maintaining a sense of humor, laughter can be one of the best coping mechanisms we have at our disposal. We've earned the right to laugh at ourselves, so why not loosen up and quit taking ourselves so seriously. Even though life can, at times, remind us that we are getting older, learn to look at the aging process as an opportunity, not an obstacle to enjoy more zestful living.

Of course, no one can discount the importance of one's genetic composition. If we're fortunate to have some of those anti-aging genes, they can certainly help us along the way. Yet, even without a genetic advantage, we can still make the right choices that will help us as we get older. So, choose to work out, decide to eat the right kind of foods, laugh more, and maintain a positive outlook, and you will likely increase your chances of making it to the impressive centenarian club.

We all are lucky to be alive. Great strides in healthcare and nutrition are being made regularly, so reaching the age of 100 is now more common than ever before. Much of the aging process can be linked to one's belief system. Begin to change your thinking that yes, it is possible to reach the elite 100 level. The possibility does exist, so examine your attitudes about the aging process. Too many of us cast our lot to a belief that we have little or no control over our destiny. With the growing number of people in triple-digits, the path has been made and the process is becoming more and more apparent. If so many others have done it, then why can't we?

William James wrote about the importance of believing how our lives can be shaped by our attitudes of mind:

> Be not afraid of life. Believe that life is worth living, and your belief
> will help create the fact.

Beliefs about longevity remind me a great deal of the classic story of the "four-minute mile." As you probably recall, at one time, it was considered to be impossible for a human being to run a mile in less than four minutes. At that time, most track and field stars, medical experts, and the general public believed that the human body was not meant to achieve that level of performance, that it was a barrier that no one would ever be capable of breaking.

Of course, that myth was shattered by Roger Bannister when, on May 6, 1954, he achieved the distinction of being the first to achieve the four-minute mile in recorded history. His record lasted only about forty days, when another runner bested his time. A previously insurmountable barrier is a common occurrence today.

The same holds true for our belief systems about growing older. Chart your own course like Roger Bannister did. Refuse to listen to the skeptics who claim that we have no control over the aging process. Study the lifestyles of people who are still active well into advanced age. You should be able to identify patterns and habits that can be adopted by just about anyone. Often, the only barriers we set upon ourselves are self-imposed and based on limited thinking or negative outlooks that can be readily changed. Look at your own life as something that you can to a great extent control. Make the decision to effectively maintain your health, your mind, and your attitude, and look for ways that you can add months and years to your life.

Remember:

> It all starts with desire; the drive to be the best. Fueled by my faith in my training, I will overcome all obstacles. I am brave! I am not afraid to face anyone on the track. I believe this is not a dream. It is my reality.

> —Roger Bannister

PLANNING TO RETIRE?

Before you make that decision that you are ready to retire, or perhaps someone else thinks you should retire, you may want to keep in mind the career of Mr. Burdette W. Andrews. According to an article in *Education Week*:[13]

> Burdette W. Andrews, who is likely the nation's oldest still serving superintendent, plans to retire from the 1,200 student Vandercook Lake public schools in Michigan, at the end of this month. Mr. Andrews, 94, has been on the job since 1946.

Over the years, the superintendent has occasionally met to share memories and lunch with a local senior citizens' group: the 31-member Vandercook Lake Class of 1947, the first graduating class during his tenure, whose members are now in their 70s.

Imagine someone retiring at the age of 94. What a terrific example that a person's age makes no difference. Many times, our only limitations are those that we place on ourselves. Our barriers are merely mentally based on the attitude we have created. I suggest that you look out for role models of longevity and use them as examples of how age had no bearing on staying active. Keep in mind Penn State football coach Joe Paterno, entertainers George Burns, Bob Hope, and Sid Caesar, broadcasters Paul Harvey and Harry Reasoner, sports commentator Jim McKay, pro football coach Dick Vermeil, fast-food franchiser Col. Harland Sanders, and Wal-Mart founder Sam Walton. I am sure you can think of many more.

You might have read about the Green Thumb organization, now known as Experience Works. Their annual award recognizes "America's Oldest Worker." According to their website (www.experienceworks.org):

> Experience Works is a national, nonprofit organization that provides training and employment services for mature workers. Established in 1965 as Green Thumb, and renamed Experience Works in 2002, the organization reaches more than 125,000 mature individuals. In addition to operating the Senior Community Service Employment Program, it provides staffing services, training programs, and Geezer.com, an e-commerce website featuring senior-made products.
>
> Each year, a national search is launched to find "America's Oldest Worker." These awards are an effort to raise awareness of the contributions made by older individuals and to break down barriers associated with the hiring of older workers.

How about these award-winning educators who were recent winners of their respective state's version of the Outstanding Older Workers award:

- Fran Trentham, age 69, Assistant to the Dean of Students at Corwder College in Neosho, Missouri
- Marvin Schlaffer, age 82, Director of Osher Lifelong Learning Institute Rutgers University in Kendall Park, New Jersey

- Louise Carpenter, age 92, School Aide at St. Andrews School in Newton, Pennsylvania
- Ella Mae Flipping, age 65, Teacher and Owner of Benevolent Child Care and Learning Center in Milwaukee, Wisconsin

These award winners are excellent examples to consider as you find yourself contemplating whether you should consider an early retirement from teaching. Remember, age need not be a factor, and it has no bearing on one's teaching ability. Use these inspirational examples as a means of motivating yourself to maintain your energy level and to reignite your passion for teaching.

These examples can also serve as reminders that oftentimes the only limitations associated with age are the ones we place on ourselves. Break out of any negative, preconceived notions you may have about age. If you're wondering that maybe you are too old to teach, forget about it, and use these examples as reminders and as a source of inspiration to keep going.

And if you're still not convinced that age has no bearing on teaching, consider the example of Hazel Haley. According to an Associated Press article,[14] the 86-year-old Haley is still teaching at Lakeland High School, the same school where she received her diploma in 1933. The headline read, "Love of students motivates state's longest-serving teacher." If Hazel Haley is still going strong at 86, then so can you. Your passion can make it happen.

9

SUMMARY AND COMMENTARY

Throughout the pages of this book, I strove to inspire you to pursue your potential and explore the greatness that lies within you. Now more than ever, you will need to tap into the reserves of your unlimited human potential to thrive and survive in today's educational arena. Always remember the potential that exists within you is often lying dormant.

My objective in writing this book is to acknowledge the fact that never before in the history of our country's school systems has there ever been such close scrutiny and open-season-type of attacks on the teaching profession. As I stressed throughout the book, much of the criticism is unfounded, unjustified, and unwarranted. Much of the criticism comes from an uninformed populace that doesn't have a clue of what it is like to teach in today's schools. Nevertheless, you need to be able to hold your head high, maintain your dignity and self-respect, persevere, and become the teacher you want to be and are destined to be.

Please plan on reviewing chapters of this book that have special meaning or significance to you. Keep this book handy and refer to it as a handbook to assist you with your endeavors, dilemmas, and, of course, to affirm and reinforce your triumphs and accomplishments as well.

I am still determined to be cheerful and happy, in whatever situation I may be; for I have also learned from experience that the greater part of our happiness or misery depends upon our dispositions, and not upon our circumstances.

—Martha Washington (former First Lady)

Despite all of the difficulties you have as a teacher, it is my hope that you can continue to develop and maintain a positive mental attitude. As you look at making it through another school year, always remember the importance of your attitude and disposition. In addition to feeling better and experiencing more positive results, positive thinking can also help you to maintain better overall health.

There is a major movement in this country that deals with positive psychology and positive expectancy. I'm convinced that positive thinking can help you age successfully. And I'm also convinced that a positive attitude can help you in the classroom as well. There is a new and emerging science that affirms that a positive attitude is more than just a state of mind. There is more and more evidence that proves the connection between attitude and well-being. An optimistic outlook can improve more than just the mental part of our being. A better attitude can lead and contribute to an improved overall physical state. The mental attitude that we choose to maintain has a linkage to what else is going on in the brain and with the mind–body connection. Therefore, I urge you to do all you can to develop and maintain a positive attitude about yourself, your school, your students, and the teaching profession.

Everyone who remembers his own educational experience remembers teachers, not methods and techniques. The teacher is the kingpin of the educational situation. He makes or breaks programs.

—Sidney Hook

I am always ready to learn, but I do not always like to be taught.

—Winston Churchill

During this decade of change and reform, I have not seen much of any mention or reference on the importance of student effort and the learner's work ethic. I believe there has been a drastic change and substantial decrease with the motivation levels, self-discipline, effort, and work ethic of many of our school children. This missing piece of success in school has been overlooked by many of the reformists. Instead of pointing fingers at and blaming teachers, the time has come for this topic to be more fully broached. I've always said that learning is a two-way street. The combined effort of both the teacher and student is an important partnership that is necessary for learning to occur.

As the school year begins, the classroom teacher is faced with dozens and dozens of human beings who come to school in varying degrees of ability, potential, maturity, motivation levels, and readiness to learn, with various health and nutrition factors, family stability (and mainly instability), neighborhood influences, and differing socioeconomic levels. The classroom is *not* a factory floor where uniformity can be molded into just one final finished product. The school is *not* an assembly line that can mass-produce exact templates of finished products meeting the same exact predetermined standard.

A POSITIVE CHANGE: MOMENTUM GAINING ON TEACHER RECOGNITION

Recently, I have noticed an increased effort to provide the teaching profession with a greater degree of respect and recognition. I believe the time has come for us to look at what's "right" with our schools, rather than what's "wrong." There are thousands of success stories waiting to be told and we need to proclaim them proudly and boldly. Stand tall and be proud, don't let the critics judge you unfairly.

For example, there are many national, state, and local "teacher of the year awards" and many teacher recognition programs sponsored by retail stores, cable television companies, and major professional sport leagues. More and more examples of teacher accolades are occurring. Many local television stations award "golden apple" salutes and national entertainment companies now have a variety of teacher recognition type awards and contests.

One particular organization that I am impressed with is Teachers-Count. According to their website (www.teacherscount.org):

> TeachersCount is a national nonprofit 501-(c) (3) organization whose mission is to raise the status of the teaching profession and providing resources to the education community. Using a public service announcement national ad campaign and related initiatives, this group is working to create a permanent culture of teacher appreciation in the United States.

How refreshing—therefore, I urge you to browse their website to find out more about this pro-teacher organization. In fact, I proudly display on all of my vehicles, their car magnet that reads, "Support America's Teachers."

Above all, stay focused, maintain your beliefs in why you became a teacher in the first place and concentrate on the value that you are adding to society by serving as a teacher. Despite all of the hardships and difficulties, teaching is still worth it. You are making a difference and incrementally you are adding value to society. Stand tall, be proud, and maintain pride in what you do. You are making a positive difference!

ONE LAST ASSIGNMENT: GIVE YOUR TEACHERS AN A+

By John Kelly, Thursday, June 14, 2007

If you can read this, thank a teacher.

If you can calculate a 15-percent tip, thank a teacher.

If you can find B flat on a clarinet, thank a teacher.

If you know how an oxbow lake forms or what photosynthesis is or what the green light in "The Great Gatsby" symbolizes, thank a teacher.

If you can speak intelligently about the causes of the Civil War or understand the passé composé or figure out the molarity of a sodium chloride solution, thank a teacher.

Thank a teacher, because you weren't born knowing this stuff. You were once a blank slate—a tabula rasa—and a teacher filled you in.

Thank a teacher if you know what tabula rasa means. Or in medias res. Or deus ex machina.

We don't really thank teachers enough, do we? And yet I can't think of people more vital to our future. You might be sitting in the Pentagon right now, directing some aspect of the global war on terrorism. You might be in an operating room, performing liposuction. You might be dribbling a basketball in the NBA Finals. You might be doing something *really, really important*, but I have news for you: What you're doing isn't as important—as sacred, as noble—as teaching a child.

Or as hard. Can you imagine standing in front of 25 or 30 kids all day, every day? And not just standing in front of them, but *teaching* them, molding their malleable little brains. You'd have to pay me to do that. (But evidently not too much. Shouldn't teachers earn as much as, say, newspaper columnists?)

Granted, you've had some bad teachers. You've had teachers who were barely a chapter ahead of you in the textbook. You've had teachers who failed to recognize your innate wonderfulness. There are people who aren't cut out to be teachers, just as there are people who shouldn't be architects or ballet dancers.

But you've had some good teachers, too. If you're lucky, you've had one or two great ones, teachers who were enthusiastic about their calling, who inspired you, who made you *understand*.

It must be tough to be a teacher these days. First, there are the parents who don't impose any discipline whatsoever on their kids and expect schools to make up for the neglect that children suffer at home. Then there are the anxious, overinvolved parents, the ones who say, "My child is gifted and talented" out of one corner of their mouths then ask out of the other: "Why are you giving him so much homework?"

Today is the last day of school for my kids. I have something to say to their teachers at Eastern Middle School and Richard Montgomery High School—and to their preschool and elementary teachers and to my teachers from all those years ago.

Thank you.[15]

APPENDIX

REFERENCE QUOTES
AND WORKSHEET

It is amazing how many quotes deal with education, teaching, and learning. This section is a collection of famous quotes that are regarded as classic accolades to teachers. If you regularly review this selection, you will continually be reminded of the important work that you do. You might even gain a new perspective on your work and the essential nature of your role as a teacher. You can renew your enthusiasm and refresh your spirit to continue to make the necessary effort to keep the momentum as you plan and deliver yet another lesson.

As you read the following quotes, keep a highlighter pen handy and mark those of special significance to you. Refer to them often. In fact, you may even want to use them as a source for your daily affirmation to establish a repetitive, familiar reminder about the profound influence you have on your students.

> A teacher affects eternity: no one can tell where his influence stops.
>
> —Henry Adams

> The object of education is to prepare the young to educate themselves throughout their lives.
>
> —Robert Maynard Hutchins

From the very beginning of his education, the child should experience the joy of discovery.

—Alfred North Whitehead

The true aim of everyone who aspires to be a teacher should be, not to impart his own opinion, but to kindle minds.

—Frederick W. Robertson

The mediocre teacher tells.
The good teacher explains.
The superior teacher demonstrates.
The great teacher inspires.

—William Arthur Ward

The whole art of teaching is only the art of awakening the natural curiosity of young minds for the purpose of satisfying it afterwards.

—Anatole France, French writer

Teachers open the door, but you must enter by yourself.

—Ancient Chinese proverb

Education is not the filling of a pail, but the lighting of a fire.

—William Butler Yeats, Irish poet

Education is not preparation for life; education is life itself.

—John Dewey, American educator

Teaching is the profession that created and spawned all other professions!
Without our precious teachers, there simply would be no other professions!
It is our teachers who have made the other professions possible.

—Tom Staszewski

In teaching you cannot see the fruit of a day's work. It is invisible and remains so, maybe for twenty years.

—Jacques Barzun, French educator

I touch the future, I teach.

—Astronaut/Teacher Christa McAuliffe

A teacher is the child's third parent.

—Hyman Maxwell Berston, American educator

Everywhere the task of teaching is the same—this lighting of sparks, this setting aflame—and everywhere it is carried on differently. This is the inherent fascination of the subject.

—Joseph Epstein

My heart is singing for joy this morning. A miracle has happened! The light of understanding has shone upon my little pupil's mind, and behold, all things are changed!

—Annie Sullivan

The illiterate of the 21st century will not be those who cannot read and write, but those who cannot learn, unlearn, and relearn.

—Alvin Toffler, author

To me, the sole hope of human salvation lies in teaching.

—George Bernard Shaw

To teach is to learn twice over.

—Joseph Joubert, French writer

It is the supreme art of the teacher to awaken joy in creative expression and knowledge.

—Albert Einstein

They who educate children well are more to be honored than they who produce them; for these only gave them life, those the art of living well.

—Aristotle

We should honor our teachers more than our parents, because while our parents cause us to live, our teachers cause us to live well.

—Philoxenus, Greek poet

The teacher's art consists in this: To turn the child's attention from trivial details and to guide his thoughts continually towards relations of importance which he will one day need to know, that he may judge rightly of good and evil in society.

—Jean-Jacques Rousseau, Philosopher

Education is the movement from darkness to light.

—Allan Bloom, educator and writer

To live is to think.

—Cicero

Teachers not only create a desire for thought, they give a student experience in thinking.

—John Sloan Dickey

What office is there which involves more responsibility, which requires more qualifications, and which ought, therefore, to be more honorable than that of teaching?

—Harriett Martineau

Only the educated are free.

—Epictetus

Education, beyond all other devices of human origin, is the great equalizer of the conditions of men—the balance-wheel of the social machinery.

—Horace Mann

Education means capacity for further education.

—John Dewey

An education isn't how much you have committed to memory. It's knowing where to go to find out what you need to know, and it's knowing how to use the information you get.

—William Feather

Education should convert the mind into a living fountain and not a reservoir.

—John M. Mason

I am still learning.

—Michelangelo

Life is a series of lessons that must be lived to be understood.

—Ralph Waldo Emerson

Students welcome any change from routine.

—William Glasser, M.D.

All students can learn.

—Charles Morley

If you are too tired to exercise, then you are probably tired because you do not exercise. Being physically fit can help you teach more effectively.

—Tom Staszewski

The function of education is to teach one to think intensively and to think critically. Intelligence plus character—that is the goal of true education.

—Martin Luther King, Jr.

Whether you think you can or think you can't, you're right.

—Henry Ford

The important thing is not so much that every child should be taught, as that every child should be given the wish to learn.

—John Lubbock, author and financier

Knowledge is the antidote to fear.

—Ralph Waldo Emerson

To love what you do and feel that it matters—how could anything be more fun?

—Katherine Graham, newspaper publisher

Teachers are expected to reach unattainable goals with inadequate tools. The miracle is that at times they accomplish this impossible task.

—Haim G. Ginott, child psychologist

Education is the soul of a society as it passes from one generation to another.

—G. K. Chesterton, author

The only medicine for suffering, crime, and all the other woes of mankind, is wisdom.

—T. H. Huxley, writer

The roots of education are bitter, but the fruit is sweet.

—Aristotle

It is only the ignorant who despise education.

—Pubilius Syrus, Latin scholar

The business of teaching is carried forward . . . because some individuals of extraordinary vitality and strength of personality engage in it, and the fire that helps to guide them kindles the spirits of the young people whose lives they touch.

—President Woodrow Wilson

Once children learn how to learn, nothing is going to narrow their minds.

—Horace Mann

The goal of education is to replace an empty mind with an open mind.

—Malcolm Forbes, publisher

Let us think of education as the means of developing our greatest abilities, because in each of us there is a private hope and dream, fulfilled, can be translated into benefit and greater strength for our nation.

—President John F. Kennedy

What greater or better gift can we offer the republic than to teach and instruct our youth.

—Marcus T. Cicero

A student won't care how much you know until he knows how much you care.

—Jaime Escalante, award winning math teacher

These are just some of my favorites. There are hundreds of them. I'm sure you can find a few of your own. You might notice that I included a couple of my own.

Now it's your turn—time for you to create *your own quote*. Why limit yourself to only reading quotes from scholars, famous people, and prominent individuals? As a practicing teacher, you already are a famous person, for it is you who provides the most important service to our society, you are the one who is entrusted to teach our young people and mold their minds to become productive citizens of our society. I cannot think of a nobler task. Since this is your book, your own thoughts and philosophy should be a part of it. On the lines below, write your own quote(s) about the art of teaching. Reflect on your viewpoints about teaching and learning, and develop your own "immortal" quotation.

_____
_____
_____
_____
_____

_____
By:_____
Date:_____
Create another, when you are able:

_____
_____
_____
_____
_____

_____
By:_____
Date:_____

Start using your own quotes in your daily routine. Using your own quotes can help you apply your own philosophy of education in your job and make it a more meaningful experience.

Remember to review these quotes on a regular basis. They can serve to verify that your work doesn't go unnoticed and that your influence is never-ending. Another side benefit is that these quotes can serve as a means of diffusing some of the negativity that you hear or receive from the critics of today's schools.

ENDNOTES

1. Rhodes, "Teachers pay for own classroom supplies," *Erie Times News*, March 9, 2002.

2. The U.S. Department of Labor's, *Dictionary of Occupational Titles*, 4th ed., 1991.

3. Ann Landers column, *Erie Times News*, March 20, 2002.

4. Irwin S. Kirsch, Ann Jungeblut, Lynn Jenkins, and Andrew Kolstad. (1993). Adult Literacy in America: a first look at the findings of the National Adult Literacy Survey (NCES 93275). U.S. Department of Education.

5. Tom Monzo, Letter to the Editor, *Penn Trafford News*, Pittsburgh, Pennsylvania.

6. Linda Shaw, "The First Year," *Seattle Times*, April 24, 2002.

7. Abraham Maslow's Hierarchy of Needs Pyramid. *Motivation and Personality*. New York: Harper, 1954.

8. "George Lucas: Creating an Empire," Arts and Entertainment Channel, December 2003.

9. Norman Cousins, *Anatomy of an Illness,* W. W. Norton. New York, 1979.

10. *Patch Adams*, Universal Studios, 1998.

11. See the Laughing Clubs website at www.laughingyoga.org.

12. Carlos Santana, *American Music Awards*, 2000.

13. Marianne Hurst, "People in the News," *Education Week*, March 27, 2002. The American Education Reform Council information homepage at www.schoolchoiceinfo.org is no longer available online.

14. Love of students motivates state's longest-serving teacher. Associated Press. November 28, 2002. http://archives.cnn.com/2002/EDUCATION/11/28/beloved.teacher.ap/index.html.

15. John Kelly, One last assignment: Give your teachers an A+, *Washington Post*, June 14, 2007.

ABOUT THE AUTHOR

Dr. Tom Staszewski (pronounced Sta-SHEF-ski) has been an educator since 1974. His career has spanned a variety of levels, from teaching elementary and middle school grades to instructing and holding various administrative positions at both the undergraduate and graduate education levels. He is presently academic dean of Mercyhurst College North East in North East, Pennsylvania.

Tom's credentials include a doctorate degree from the University of Pittsburgh in Administrative and Policy Studies, a master's degree from Indiana University of Pennsylvania in Adult and Community Education, and a bachelor's from Penn State University in Elementary Education. He possesses a permanent (active) state teaching certificate (grades K–8).

In addition, Tom has an extensive background in staff development, consulting, and training and is actively involved in providing professional development services for teachers, school districts, and educational organizations.

He resides in his hometown of Erie, Pennsylvania, with his wife, Linda. Tom is a firm believer in the "magic of human potential and believes that each student has great talents and abilities." He believes that not all students are good test takers, but that all students can learn and succeed—they just learn differently and they should be evaluated using a multitude of authentic assessment methods.

The author can be contacted at tomstasz@verizon.net